BELLA ABZUG

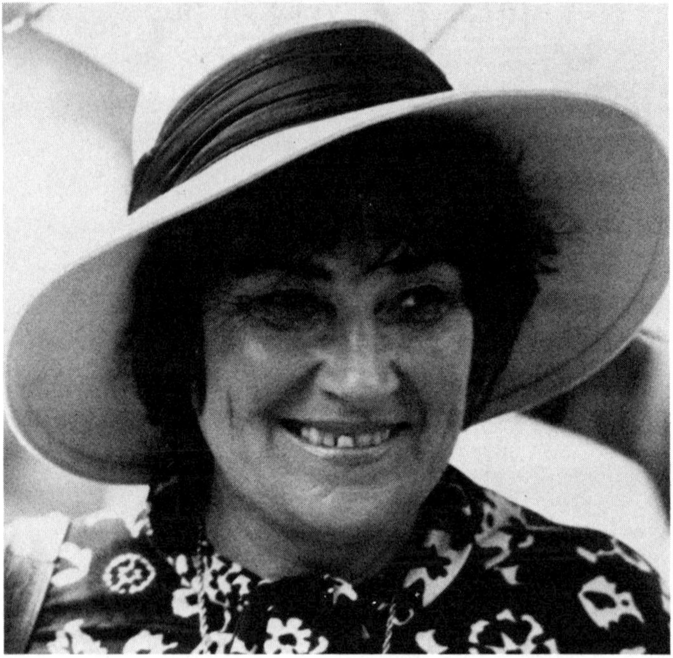

BELLA ABZUG

Doris Faber

Illustrated with photographs

Lothrop, Lee & Shepard Company
A Division of William Morrow & Company, Inc.
New York

Also by Doris Faber

Oh, Lizzie! The Life of Elizabeth Cady Stanton

Petticoat Politics:
How American Women Won the Right to Vote

I Will Be Heard:
The Life of William Lloyd Garrison

The Perfect Life: The Shakers in America

Copyright © 1976 by Doris Faber

All rights reserved. No part of this book may be reproduced or utilized in any form or by any means, electronic or mechanical, including photocopying, recording or by any information retrieval system, without permission in writing from the Publisher. Inquiries should be addressed to Lothrop, Lee and Shepard Company, 105 Madison Ave., New York, N. Y. 10016. Printed in the United States of America.
1 2 3 4 5 6 7 8 9 10

Library of Congress Cataloging in Publication Data

Faber, Doris (date)
  Bella Abzug.
  Bibliography: p.
  Includes index.
  SUMMARY: A biography of Congresswoman Bella Abzug who has crusaded for peace, civil liberties, and women's rights.
  1. Abzug, Bella S., 1920- —Juvenile literature. [1. Abzug, Bella., 1920- 2. Legislators] I. Title.
E840.8.A2F3   328.73′092′4 [B]   76-21869
ISBN 0-688-41776-0   ISBN 0-688-51776-5 lib. bdg.

Acknowledgments

Most of the photographs that appear in this book have been provided by members of Bella Abzug's staff or her family, and the author is extremely grateful to them as well as to the photographers and picture services whose prints are reproduced with their permission. For permission to quote copyrighted material, thanks are also due to the *Washington Post*, the *Wall Street Journal*, and the *Chicago Tribune*.

Contents

1   "Isn't She Something!"   3
2   The Way It Was   10
3   Two Schools   21
4   Martin—and Law   31
5   Three Lives   44
6   Mount Vernon   56
7   From Peace to Politics   68
8   "This Woman's Place..."   82
9   Rocking the Boat   95
10   Exit?   112
11   Back on the Hill   129
12   And What Next?   148
Suggested for Further Reading   157
Index   159

A Note of Thanks

To Bella Abzug, first, for grinning and bearing so many questions when there was so much else demanding her attention, and to Martin Abzug whose help has been beyond measure, just as his wife often says it is; to Dora Friedman, Mim Kelber, Lee Novick and the others on the Abzug staff who patiently interrupted their own work whenever I called on them; and also to all of the former newspaper colleagues and friends and political figures who most obligingly gave me assistance of various sorts while I was gathering the material for this book.

But there wouldn't have been any book without Chaucy Bennetts, the editor who had the idea that there ought to be one and who has provided constant encouragement and enthusiasm. So I must say a special word of thanks to her for involving me in such a fascinating adventure—as well as to my own family who have put up with endless talk on the same topic during these past months. For everybody wanted to know: What's Bella really like? I do hope that readers will find their answer in the pages that follow.

D.F.

BELLA ABZUG

1

"Isn't She Something!"

Room B-364, the slip says.

If you're a stranger on Capitol Hill, you soon get lost in the maze of basement corridors that connect the massive buildings where members of Congress conduct the nation's business. At last you find a uniformed guard and ask directions. He shakes his head. That's off limits to visitors, you're told.

But you're lucky enough to have a special pass, so you're steered toward the right area. As you've been led to expect, there is a panel of glass allowing you to see into this room from the hallway. One glance, and you relax. For Bella has not arrived yet.

Bella Abzug, that is. Congresswoman Bella S. Abzug of New York. But everybody in Washington seems to call her just Bella, and even though you don't really know her, you feel as if you do.

You've met her only briefly up in her office a few hours earlier, before she rushed out to several appointments. Instantly, though, she reminded you of your favorite aunt—the same glint of mischief in her eyes, the same warm tone to her voice. She's also much better-looking than her pictures; on the heavy side, no doubt about it, but very stylish with one of her famous hats of a soft beige that just matches the background of her diamond-printed dress. Now you're eager to watch her in action, and to hear her, too, if this television crew will let you.

For Room B-364 is a TV studio, set up in the Capitol basement to save time for busy lawmakers. Staring through the glass panel, you notice that the far end is arranged like an office, and near the desk stands a wooden pole of the sort usually used for hanging coats. But on this particular morning the hooks hold hats instead—a wide-brimmed black straw hat, a similar item in tan felt, another of bright red. You can see about a dozen people fiddling with lights or pieces of paper, or staring anxiously at a clock on the wall.

Suddenly, there's commotion in the corridor. Along comes Bella, striding with head and shoulders bent forward as if she would rather be running. Several younger men and women follow after her. You feel a tremor of excitement, and it appears that even the TV people feel the same way.

Isn't She Something!

The cameraman, the producer, the talk-show hostess, they all surge toward the door. They are used to working with celebrities, yet they stand gaping like ordinary tourists. You guess that they must be wondering: What's Bella going to say today? For you've already gathered from some of her staff that Bella is full of surprises; she can be funnier than Carol Burnett, she can charm a snake when she wants to be charming, and she can terrify a lion when she gets angry. So it's never boring around Congresswoman Bella Abzug.

The subject of so much attention winks when she sees you, and waves for you to walk along with her.

"How did I get into this?" she asks one and all as she strides through the door. "I have no makeup on." With an elaborate sigh, she rummages in her purse for a mirror, then proceeds to apply a little lipstick, all the while keeping up a grumbling routine she is clearly enjoying.

"What program is this anyway? You mean, just a *Washington* station? Well, who the—I won't say what you think I was going to say. But I don't have the time to do a Washington show—"

The beautiful black woman who is the show's hostess dares to interrupt and explain that this is part of a series of interviews featuring each of the women members of Congress.

"I'll bet they're all more cooperative than me," Bella says, and she puts on a comic scowl. The hostess gulps to try to keep from laughing as she goes on to describe the special gimmick of this interview series, which is to present each of the women Representatives with a portrait of herself painted by a woman artist. Somebody else brings over the painting of Bella Abzug. "Isn't it pretty?" the hostess asks.

"I don't think so," Bella announces after barely glancing at the picture. "I think I'm prettier than that." Then she pats on a touch of rouge while her hostess gamely defends the merits of the painting. A minute later, Bella snaps her purse closed. "Here, let me see that picture," she demands.

The Congresswoman takes the canvas, peers at it and shakes her head. "Look at that hard face," she says. "Oh, that's terrible!" Then she beams upon her hostess. "Now look how sweet and gentle I am."

The hostess is laughing too hard to be able to reply. "Are you going to say that when I present the picture?" she finally gasps. Bella nods with the utmost good humor. "I don't like to insult artists, though," she adds. "My daughter is a sculptor." Her eyes narrow as she notes her hats on the rack beside the desk. "I hope you're going to return my hats to their proper place," she remarks. "All right, let's get this over with."

Ordinarily, it's the task of the hostess to ease her guest into a relaxed frame of mind before a taping session starts. Yet this guest apparently makes her own rules. "Isn't she something!" an Abzug aide murmurs.

Then some bright lights are switched on, the guest

and hostess seat themselves in leather chairs that have been placed a few feet in front of the desk, a camera whirrs, and a composed voice says, "Good morning, I'm Carole Simpson of NBC News and today the Sunday Show is happy to present one of the most controversial members of this Congress . . ."

As smoothly as if every word had been rehearsed, Carole Simpson asks her first question: "Congresswoman Abzug, how many hats do you have?" Bella Abzug grins a private grin as if she's thinking about how rich she'd be if she had a dime for every time she's been asked that, but she just answers that these days she doesn't have too many because fund-raising organizations keep requesting one to auction off for some worthy cause. "I keep only about half a dozen to a dozen on hand."

And where does she get them?

Well, she has a friend who's a designer, and as to which hat she picks out on any given morning, that depends on how she happens to feel that day.

But how did she become so partial to hats?

Very simple. Back in the days when she was a young lawyer, there were not so many women lawyers, and when she turned up on a case, somebody would always assume that she was a secretary or errand girl, and so she got the idea that wearing a hat would make her look more important, more like a professional person. Anyway, she'd always liked hats; she supposed they were part of her identity.

Identity. Carole Simpson likes that word, and she

uses it to lead into the main part of the interview. Bella Abzug has become a national figure, unlike most members of Congress. Not only in her own New York City district, but all over the country, she is known not just as a very colorful political personality, but also for her strong stand on many issues, like peace and women's rights. She has a definite political identity. When you say Bella Abzug, everybody knows who you mean. What's gone into the making of Bella Abzug?

The Congresswoman hesitates barely an instant, then begins:

"I'm fifty-five years old and I've always been a very concerned citizen . . ."

She talks for a minute or two, her voice growing more earnest as she mentions some of the kinds of change she has been fighting to achieve. Yet this is just a short interview, and she has clearly learned a lot about television as well as about politics. So she stops talking in plenty of time to allow for the presentation of that picture—and, despite her off-camera threat, she compromises. She politely thanks the artist, merely adding with a wicked grin that she's seen better pictures of herself.

Off go the bright lights, and the television crew seems vastly relieved. While they are still congratulating each other about how well the show went, Congresswoman Abzug grabs her purse and heads for the door. She's had three committee meetings already this morning, she has another session on New York City's financial crisis in another hour, she's got a sheaf of yellow slips an aide has just handed her, each with a very urgent message—

But what *has* gone into the making of Bella Abzug?

2

The Way It Was

In the Bronx, in the 1920's, there were empty lots every few blocks where kids could play ball. Up around the reservoir, Bella Savitzky could even ride a bike on a grassy path without having to watch for autos. While nobody from Kansas would have called this part of New York City countrified, Bella would always remember it as nice and open.

She'd been born in a less pleasant neighborhood, on July 24, 1920. "It's an interesting date," she liked to tell people long afterward, when she began making political speeches. "That's the year the women of the United States won the right to vote." However, plain survival was more important than politics on the kind of street Bella's earliest memories recall.

Bella at five. *Courtesy of Martin Abzug*

This was in the East Bronx, later to beome one of the worst slums imaginable. Although the area had a much less fearful fame then, it was already crowded and grimy. Yet Bella's father would often say they should count their blessings, that compared with his own first home in America, down on the city's Lower East Side, here was a paradise.

Even so, as soon as he possibly could, Emanuel Savitzky rented a clean apartment for his family near the last stop on the subway, not far from the Kingsbridge reservoir. In this section, there were still some small houses where a single family lived all by itself. To Bella, the idea of such luxury was fantastic, but she also wondered if it wouldn't be lonesome having no close neighbors. Anyway, only rich people could afford their own house, and her father was definitely not a rich man.

He was a butcher, and his shop was almost an hour by subway to Manhattan's Ninth Avenue. If he ever got tired of this trip twice a day, he never said so, but Manny Savitzky never said a cross or angry word on any subject. He was probably the most peace-loving man alive, he himself would often brag with a twinkle in his eye. Hadn't he left Russia as a young fellow back in 1905 to protest when his country went to war against Japan? But by the time Bella was about ten, she'd learned there was more to the story than that.

For in Russia, Jewish people like them had frequently been treated with awful cruelty. Her own mother had grown up there, and when she was

Esther Tanklefsky, a lovely girl with braids of shiny dark hair and sparkling dark eyes, she had seen Russian soldiers roughly seize Jewish young men and drag them from their families. In some villages, Jewish women and children had been viciously stabbed to death for no crime other than following their religion. Happily, Grandpa and Grandma Tanklefsky had managed to escape with their children to America not so long after Emanuel Savitzky—and tens of thousands of other Jewish refugees—had sought freedom in the New World.

Manny Savitzky did have some basis, though, for his good-natured boasting about being especially peaceable. Just a few years before Bella was born, while her sister Helene was a baby, the United States had been drawn into the great World War overwhelming Europe. Once the fighting ended, President Woodrow Wilson tried hard to win approval for his fourteen-point peace program. But statesmen and ordinary citizens on both sides of the Atlantic had soon got to quibbling about various of those points, to the disgust of a mild-tempered butcher.

There was an easy way to solve the whole situation, he insisted. So one morning he got a bucket of paint, climbed a ladder, and offered his own plan for world peace on the sign above his shop. This was what he painted:

THE LIVE AND LET LIVE MEAT MARKET

He just couldn't grasp why some people laughed at his sign, or tried to tell him the slabs of beef in his window didn't look alive, thank God. Of course not, but why joke about it? Young as she was, Bella could sense that her father might have liked some other business better, or no business at all. For it was scarcely a secret that he loved listening to music, and a special glow lit his face when he played one of his Enrico Caruso records on the Victrola. Because of him, the whole family shared a marvelous bond.

Every Friday evening, after the lighting of the Sabbath candles and the saying of the Sabbath prayers, and after the feast Bella's mother and grandmother had spent all day preparing, their small living room would turn into a private concert hall. With his fine tenor voice, Bella's father would lead everyone in singing his favorite folk songs, while Helene accompanied them on the piano and Bella did her best with her violin.

Those Sabbath evenings gave her a feeling of warmth she would never forget. Besides her parents and her sister, Grandma and Grandpa Tanklefsky lived with them, as did a bachelor brother of her mother's. No doubt he helped out by paying them a little money every week, but all Bella knew about money in this carefree period was that they didn't have much—and still they weren't poor, like some of their neighbors.

Of course they were somewhat crowded, with seven people crammed into an old-style apartment of dim and tiny rooms. What did that matter? They laughed, they sang, they flung out their arms and danced together, or if anyone felt sad they could even enjoy crying together. So Bella would always remember being wonderfully loved and protected during her childhood, not just by her family but also by the most solemn Jehovah the Almighty.

For when she was very young, Bella had imagined a most comforting picture. Her Grandpa Tanklefsky was a handsome old man, with the white and flowing beard of a figure from the Bible, and once as she sat a bit restlessly in the synagogue during religious services, she found herself supposing Jehovah had a familiar face. Soon she stopped confusing her dear grandfather and the Supreme Being of her religion, but she still did whatever she could to please them both.

That led to a lot of questions from Bella.

She had a startling gift for memorizing, so by the age of only seven or eight she could already recite many of the Hebrew prayers she heard in the synagogue. This astounded her grandfather, and when his elderly cronies would come to visit, he would lift her up on a table, urging her to give a demonstration. How those old men would smile and fuss over her!

Naturally, Bella got the notion that she must be pretty good at learning Hebrew. And in her house, nobody ever told her girls were dumb or silly or in any way inferior to boys. So how come she had to sit up in the balcony when she went to temple?

Why couldn't she and all the other girls and

women sit downstairs with the men and boys? Why must they stay practically out of sight and never take any real part in conducting the service? Why? Why? Why?

"This is the way it is," her grandfather would say. And he would not explain any further, no matter how often she asked. But ask she did, until her mother told her to stop already, they had enough of her arguing. Yet Bella knew her mother must actually be proud of her because of the smile with which she informed everybody about what was wrong with this daughter.

"She came out yelling," Mrs. Savitzky said, and she laughed.

So Bella knew her mother was just pretending to be annoyed and that underneath she liked to hear Bella speak up. Since their religion meant such a lot in this household, Bella would never forget this early feeling of being treated unfairly. Years later, when she was invited to address Jewish gatherings, she'd inform them cheerfully, "I have a funny idea that being sent up to that balcony had something to do with my being involved the way I turned out to be." When she was only eleven, she'd started to take steps toward becoming "involved."

At the Jewish Center connected with their synagogue, where she went to Hebrew school several afternoons a week following her regular school classes, they had a bulletin board listing different activities. Some of these supported efforts in many

The Way It Was

parts of the world aimed toward establishing a Jewish homeland in Palestine. Although Bella felt no desire to settle anyplace else, she surely did believe that other people who were less fortunate ought to have that opportunity. Besides, she wanted to show that a girl could accomplish plenty in a Zionist youth group.

Before she joined, the members of the group would go over to the subway entrance about once a week and stand there shaking cardboard boxes to collect pennies for the cause. But Bella decided almost immediately that they'd get more money by boarding a train, then walking through the cars, approaching every passenger. Soon she had an even better idea.

As the train stopped at a station, the noise level suddenly got much lower. It still wasn't exactly quiet, but Bella could really shout if she wanted to—and she shouted out a little speech while the other members went up to one passenger after another, collecting coins. This system worked so well that she repeated the performance at every stop. Who said a girl couldn't be a leader?

For a while Bella was so fired up with Zionist fervor that she dreamed about going to Palestine as a young pioneer and enduring all sorts of hardship to help create green farms in the desert there. The camp she went to for several weeks in the summer was run by a Jewish educational agency, so she had another reason for being loyal to the cause. But once she got to camp, her enthusiasm would take her in other directions.

She was some tomboy, everybody told her, and she guessed it must be true. There wasn't a sport she disliked; she would go out for any game—volleyball, basketball, track and field, anything. Although her main love was swimming, she could do fine in all kinds of athletic contests, and she played to win. So when it came to choosing up sides, the other girls always wanted to be with Bella.

In fact, she couldn't help being aware that she was popular back in the Bronx, too. Whenever someone was starting up a game of Red Rover or stickball, even boys would holler to have her on their team. Not that boys were anything special; she had a shoebox full of gleaming marbles won from playing Immies with any male challenger.

As she approached high school, though, Bella did notice that some boys were hanging around her pretty often. Helene, who was nearly five years older than she was, already had a serious boy friend, but Bella thought this boy-girl business was silly. Still, she didn't exactly suffer when she passed a mirror, and yet why should she worry about how she looked? The way some other girls would talk so much on this topic was ridiculous. Besides, during the year after she turned twelve, Bella had a lot more important things to worry about.

First, it was her grandpa. They were all whispering over plans to celebrate his eightieth birthday

The Way It Was

when he took sick, and within just a few days he died. Of course, he had lived a good life, but Bella had always been able to run to him when things went wrong, so she deeply missed him.

Then a more bitter sorrow struck. Her darling father, at the age of only fifty-two, collapsed with a severe heart attack, and he did not recover. Bella could hardly believe it when they told her he was dead. Oh, how she wept!

For the first time, then, she wished that she'd been born a boy. How could she help it when all the relatives were moaning about what a shame it was that Manny didn't have a son to say the memorial prayer for him? But Bella snapped out of that particular weakness pretty quickly.

She just marched over to the synagogue early the next morning, and without paying the least attention to the staring of the men in their prayer shawls, she stood right in front of the altar, bowed her head and began to intone the solemn Hebrew words of the Kaddish. *"Yisgadal veyiskadash . . ."* "May His great name be magnified . . ." According to the Orthodox Jewish tradition, this most holy farewell was to be recited daily during a year of mourning by the close male relatives of the dear departed.

But nobody interfered with Bella, despite the fact that females were not even supposed to enter the main area of a temple. Every morning for the following year, before she went to school, Bella stopped at the synagogue to say Kaddish for her father.

Her life changed in other ways, too. Since her mother refused to consider moving in with any relatives, the problem of earning money arose. Manny Savitzky had left some insurance, but not enough for his wife and daughters to live on. So Mrs. Savitzky found work as a department-store cashier, and Helene began giving piano lessons. What could Bella do when she was barely thirteen?

She could do her share when she got a little older, her mother told her. And within a few years, Bella was teaching beginners' groups learning the Hebrew language, history, and customs at the Kingsbridge Jewish Center. Come summer, she managed to get a free vacation, besides earning a little extra, by assisting the swimming counselor at camp.

But nothing interfered with Bella's own schooling—her mother wouldn't have stood for that, even if Bella had had any such notion.

3

Two Schools

The high school Bella went to was Walton, rated one of the best in the city for girls. Right in her own neighborhood, near the reservoir, it was separated from De Witt Clinton for boys by a wide stretch of athletic fields. Since not many New York high schools were co-ed then, Bella didn't see anything strange about having just girls in her classes.

Actually, sports still were her main interest. With her reddish brown hair chopped off short, she would bound around the campus in gym suit and sneakers, somewhat amazing or amusing classmates who preferred doing their competing on test papers. That didn't distress Bella. She did her homework, and she got good grades. Besides, she liked almost everybody, and almost everybody must have liked her because she got elected class president several semesters, including her senior year.

By then, she was much more concerned with what was going on in the world, and in how she could help. President Franklin D. Roosevelt and his New Deal had made a powerful impression on her. "My friends," he would say over the radio in his high-toned voice, sounding very different from anyone she ever met in the Bronx, but somehow still sounding as if he were talking directly to her about his ideas for solving the nation's problems.

Bella had been only nine when the stock market on Wall Street crashed in 1929 and hard times had spread across the country. Naturally, she'd noticed her parents shaking their heads over the bad news, but it didn't seem to have much bearing on her own life. Then after her father died, she'd had trouble enough without worrying a lot about other people's troubles.

Yet, when she was around sixteen she began wondering how she'd been so blind. Hadn't her parents taught her it was part of their religion to feel for suffering fellow humans, no matter whether they were friends or strangers? And here was the leader of the United States government, not only caring about the plight of poor people, but also taking bold steps toward improving life for the average person.

Instead of just spouting fine words, he was starting programs to provide jobs for the jobless, and to build new schools and new housing, to give new hope for everybody, young and old. His New Deal was action, not merely words, and Bella had always been in favor of doing something, rather than simply talking about it.

So by the time she graduated from Walton in January of 1938, Bella was bursting to start doing something herself. First, though, she would have to attend two more schools. For she knew exactly what she wanted to do, and it couldn't be done without a couple of more diplomas.

She wanted to be a lawyer.

Her mother thought this was a fine idea. She herself had arrived in the United States knowing not a word of English, but she'd caught up to the extent of aiming to become a teacher. However, she'd been obliged to quit school without finishing her training, so she could help out in a family business. Then, after her husband died and she had to raise their daughters alone, she kept thinking what a shame it was she hadn't been better equipped to face the world.

Her girls must have the best possible schooling, Esther Savitzky felt strongly. By all means let them choose the profession that most appealed to them, though. So if Bella had set her heart on standing up in a courtroom to defend poor people—all right, let her try it. But some of Bella's aunts and uncles definitely did not agree.

Girls weren't supposed to think about *being* a lawyer, they insisted. That was work for a man. Girls could only dream about *marrying* a lawyer; didn't she understand?

No! Bella would explode when she heard nonsense like that. For it was stupid to tell girls they should merely sit and wait until they found a man who'd support them.

So let a girl take up some ladylike way of making a little money before she got married, the relatives said. Such as teaching.

Okay, Bella granted them, okay if teaching is your goal in life. But why shouldn't a woman with the ability and the ambition to be a doctor or a lawyer have as much chance as any man?

Oh! Oh! Oh! What a lot of sputtering this kind of talk provoked. Bella sputtered right back, of course, waving her arms and making such an assortment of faces that her mother said maybe she'd better change her mind—she'd make a great actress. Still, Bella knew perfectly well that her mother was really on her side. And so was Helene, who'd already finished college and was taking advanced training in music while earning her keep giving lessons.

Anyway there was no need to carry on all this shouting, at least until another four years elapsed. Thanks to New York City's system of free colleges, everybody agreed that Bella was entitled to that much higher education. Like most of her friends at Walton, she'd just assumed that when she graduated she would move to the other side of the reservoir and attend Hunter.

Bella hadn't bargained on one fact, though. Probably because of the Depression, so many city families were sending their daughters to this fine women's college by the late 1930s, at no cost to themselves, that Hunter's leafy Bronx campus was overcrowded. A new skyscraper headquarters was rising on Park Avenue and Sixty-eighth Street, down in Manhattan. Meanwhile, makeshift classrooms had to be provided for incoming freshmen.

So Bella had to go by subway to an old factory building in the wholesale furniture district on her first day as a college student. But even there, more than an hour from home, she quickly got over feeling lost. When a sign went up announcing a meeting to elect the freshman class president, some of her friends from Walton urged her to run. Why not? Bella grasped instantly that if she could get the solid vote of her own high school's contingent, she had a good chance of winning.

It didn't bother her that there were quite a few former Walton girls she barely recognized, some of the big brains or the boy-crazy bunch. If she tried, she could easily find somebody who did know every one of them. Sure enough, a couple of days later she had organized a group of Walton grads to roam up and down the halls, grabbing people.

"Come on!" they urged. "We've got to go to a meeting. Bella's running for class president."

So she did win, and from then on her college years were a whirl of drama. During these tense years the greatest war in history erupted, making any discussion of ordinary student concerns like club dues or dances seem ridiculous. But even before the fighting broke out, Bella and her friends had such strong opinions about what was happening over in Europe and Asia that they kept bringing up a different type of question.

For instance, was it patriotic to wear silk stockings?

At that time, not even a brave individual like Bella ever came to classes in slacks, let alone jeans. Practically everybody appeared in a pleated skirt, a sweater, and a string of pearls or some other plain beads. Silk stockings were expected to cover the limited expanse of leg visible below the hem of the skirt.

Yet where did the silk in the stockings come from? Japan!

And despite Japan's menacing policies in the Far East, a deal had just been approved to send Japan vast quantities of scrap iron salvaged when the old elevated railway on Sixth Avenue in New York City had been torn down. How many bullets would all that metal make? Why shouldn't intelligent students demonstrate their disgust with Japan's militaristic policies by refusing to buy any Japanese products?

Because stockings made of the newly invented nylon were so fearfully expensive, a few classmates with no interest in world affairs had the nerve to murmur.

But Bella did far more than endure the discomfort

Two Schools 27

of lumpy cotton stockings. Especially after the dreadful spring of 1940, when the war machine of Nazi Germany overran one country after another, leaving England alone to defend democracy, she spent much of her energy arguing for decisive action by the government of the United States. By then, her class had become the first to move into Hunter's new home, and Bella Savitzky had been elected the president of the entire student body of about four thousand young women.

Knowing her just from her reputation as a political activist, incoming freshmen were astonished when they met her. For she was gorgeous! Since she'd emerged from her tomboy stage, she'd let her hair grow longer, until it was stylishly framing her face. And what a face, of cool ivory with the warmest smile imaginable, so even if she'd wanted to avoid making new friends, she would have had a hard time.

Yet she had no such aim, of course. Although she could be fierce in debate, Bella was always ready to go off to a party where she'd sit up all night puffing cigarettes and singing or strumming a mandolin.

That was fun, but she still refused to take dating seriously and she was amazed that some of her friends were flashing engagement rings or even running off to get married. Would she ever allow a man to persuade her to marry him? Well, said Bella, she'd already been asked plenty of times, but she thought it would be preposterous to give up her own plans. Maybe after she finished law school and was estab-

As president of the student council at Hunter, Bella sat on the platform when First Lady Eleanor Roosevelt addressed the college. *Courtesy of Martin Abzug*

lished in her career, if some attractive man could prove to her that they might both keep their independence...

Then she'd break into a sly smile without completing her sentence. For it did not seem terribly likely that such an ideal man existed, though she certainly had no worries on this subject. Right now, she was much too busy with other matters, especially student council meetings.

Two Schools

By more or less memorizing Robert's Rules of Order, Bella practically took charge of these meetings. Sure, there was still plenty of uproar, but she stayed very cool—and she always knew more about the various ways and means of getting a resolution adopted than anybody else did. Particularly after Pearl Harbor, when the United States finally was drawn into the actual fighting, she kept alarming the college authorities by pushing through bold statements of policy about what Congress and the White House should be doing.

Yes, she'd miss this challenge when she graduated. But during her last semester she was mainly looking forward to the new challenge of law school. Not that anybody was trying to stop her now, for once the aunts and uncles realized that she meant what she said they just shrugged and wished her luck. Actually, she was rather lucky to be applying at this point in history, though she would rather not think of it that way. Because of the war, with every able-bodied young man being grabbed by the draft, a woman student stood a much better than usual chance of being accepted by one of the top law schools.

As far as Bella was concerned, Harvard was the very top. So she applied there, but despite her high marks and the shortage of male candidates she was swiftly turned down—"We take no females," they told her.

"This is outrageous!" Bella stormed to her mother.

The thought kept going through her mind that she should do something about such a great injustice, yet what *could* she do? Maybe someday she could get a law passed, but meanwhile her mother tried to soothe her.

"You don't have the money anyway to live at Harvard," Mrs. Savitzky told her. "You know you'll have to live at home. And what's wrong with Columbia?"

Bella had to admit that Columbia, right in New York, had a very fine law school. Furthermore, they were willing to give her a scholarship that would practically pay the tuition expenses of about four hundred dollars a year. With her savings from teaching Hebrew and summer camp jobs, plus whatever she could earn working a couple of hours a day, she'd manage.

Of course, she'd still be commuting by subway and that was exhausting. During her last weeks at Hunter, she began feeling terribly run-down. Besides having to face final exams, she was rushing breathlessly to hear the latest war bulletins on the radio in the student lounge several times every day, she was cramping her fingers knitting one heavy wool hat after another for the armed forces and, oh, she needed a rest.

So right after graduating, Bella boarded a train bound south—to visit her Aunt Janet and Uncle Julius who were vacationing in Florida.

4

Martin--and Law

It was on a bus, a crowded bus in Miami. Bella was riding back from a violin concert by the famed Yehudi Menuhin, and the music had thrilled her so much that she hardly noticed the nice-looking fellow staring at her. He had a seat, but she certainly didn't mind standing so she just shook her head when this fellow made a move to rise and let her sit down.

Then suddenly he was murmuring some crazy poetry into her ear.

What kind of a nut was he?

Not a bit nutty, he assured her. No, he added, maybe that wasn't true. Because he was obliged to inform her that he had already fallen for her like a ton of bricks.

So Martin Abzug made her laugh right from the

minute she met him. Of course, she hadn't the slightest interest in marrying him, a subject which he mentioned only about two minutes later. For she still didn't really know if she'd ever marry, but if she did it certainly wouldn't be till after she finished law school and was established in her profession. It might be easier then, she thought, to find a man who respected her right to have a life of her own, not just to share his.

Still, Bella couldn't help feeling touched when Martin told her that he'd been watching her all through the concert. And the silly patter he kept up while the bus swayed toward the street where her relatives were staying tickled her. So why not? She gave him her address and said he could come over the following evening.

Martin arrived clutching a box of expensive candy, which he presented, practically getting down on his knees like a character in the movies—to Aunt Janet. That went over big, at least with Bella's rich aunt whose main aim in life these days seemed to be getting this niece safely married off. But Aunt Janet had to be sure the young man was really as good a catch as he appeared to be, so, bang, bang, she bomborded him with questions, which Martin answered cheerfully.

Why, sure he was a New Yorker too; he lived with his family on West End Avenue, and he worked for his father in the garment district—they manufactured ladies' blouses. Aunt Janet cast a glance of triumph toward Uncle Julius, a wholesale butcher himself, who could easily spot another well-off individual, and Uncle Julius nodded approvingly.

No, Martin went on, maybe he ought to say he was temporarily unemployed. The relatives suddenly looked horrified, but then Martin added that being twenty-six years old and in sound health, he'd recently received greetings from everybody's Uncle Sam, so at the end of the month he was going into the army, and there were great sighs of relief.

While Bella was torn between guffawing at this whole performance, or just telling everybody to please mind their own business, she soon had to admit to herself that she was more than mildly interested by her new friend. Whether they went swimming or bike riding or sat sipping ice cream sodas, he kept coming out with remarks she thought were very funny. You never could predict what he'd say next, or what he'd do, either. One evening he announced that as long as he would be risking his neck in the service of his country by the end of the month, he was going to spend his last week of freedom taking the kind of risk he preferred. So he'd be departing in the morning to go up to Canada and do some skiing.

What? Though Bella had tried every sport she'd had the chance to, she'd never yet met anybody who went sliding down snowy hillsides on wooden slats.

She missed him more than she'd expected, but he wrote her long letters from Canada, then from the army training camp where he was sent. In addition to amusing her, he also had the nerve to lecture her. "Go to work in the defense of your country," he told her, and Bella felt somewhat surprised to find herself following his advice. Of course, she'd graduated from Hunter in January, so she wouldn't be starting at Columbia until September, giving her several months to test his idea.

She did test it soon after returning to New York by applying for a job with a firm that designed navy ships. While she was waiting to hear when to report, she signed up to demonstrate how to wrap a new style of turban around her head in a department store.

When she got home after eight hours of tying and untying that turban, she practically collapsed. "I have no arms," she moaned to her mother. So that job lasted less than a week and then she found another, grading Regents exams. In a couple of days she had more bad news for her mother. "I got fired for talking," she reported tersely.

Then her summons to start at the ship-designing firm arrived. It turned out that her mission was to fill out forms for the ordering of supplies, and all around her in a dusty office near the foot of Manhattan, the sound of staplers pounding pieces of paper together bombarded her ears. Trying to keep up her spirits, she imagined that the staplers were banging in the rhythm of the popular Latin-American conga beat. *Bang-bang, bang-bang, BANG-bang . . . bang-bang, bang-bang, BANG-bang . . .*

It was dreadfully boring, but she stayed long enough to be awarded a navy "E" for efficiency. Then one evening Bella suddenly said to her mother, "This is crazy; I'm not making any contribution to the defense of my country." Mrs. Savitzky could not dispute the point. Bella sat down then and wrote to Martin. "I'm not working up to my potential," she proclaimed. The next day she let Columbia know that she'd be starting law school in September, after all.

But as much as she'd looked forward to this, her first weeks at the high and mighty Columbia were slightly scary. Here, in a sort of private preserve off upper Broadway, was an atmosphere like none other she'd ever known. It was almost like stepping into the past. The buildings were musty old brick and the professors had the same stiff manner as the fogies in a museum painting—even the words they spoke seemed to belong to a different language.

But Bella was determined to learn this lingo, no matter how baffling some of it sounded. Until now, she'd always found that getting good marks was pretty easy, yet now she had to sit up in the law library, sometimes until one in the morning, before she made much sense out of the next day's assignment. And, barely rested, she'd be back on the subway riding downtown again by half-past seven.

It didn't help matters that, to earn a few dollars, she was also dishing out a few thousand dinners every day at one of the university dorms taken over by the navy. Wearing a gruesomely hot white uniform, she'd have to stand behind a steam tray until she thought she'd faint from heat exhaustion.

But all right, if it took all this to become a lawyer, she'd do it. Bella knew one thing for sure—she wasn't going to drop out or be dropped, either. So she put in month after month until gradually—she hardly realized it was happening—she began actually enjoying the whole routine.

Partly, she supposed, she was getting used to the stuffy air of Columbia; but also she was making the great discovery that people were people, despite a lot of outward differences. So far, she'd been mainly involved with what her family called *landsmen*, meaning that they shared the same kind of Jewish background. Oh, of course she'd known loads of non-Jews all through school, and she had friends, good friends, from Harlem and Little Italy, from all over the city. For Hunter certainly deserved being described by the words that were often used about the city itself: Hunter really was a melting pot. Yet the mixture was mostly on the poor side—nobody's father was a big banker or corporation president.

On the other hand, here at Columbia many of the students seemed to come from another world where, if you went to camp in the summer, you probably went to an expensive place up in Maine, surely not upstate to the Catskills, known for their popularity with the Jewish community. Your family had a maid, and a car, and you'd been taught all sorts of snooty manners. These New Yorkers were strange enough, but there were also many students from such mysterious territories as Ohio, along with a sprinkling of real foreigners who'd grown up in distant countries like Spain. While all this was quite interesting, in normal times it would be somewhat unfriendly here, Bella imagined.

But the times were very far from normal because of the war. Practically all of the fellows in their second or third year were racing through the required courses, hoping to get enough credits to graduate before their draft boards caught up with them. Her own class had twenty women, more than twice the usual number, and although sixty-five men had started in September, every month a few more disappeared until finally there were only about twenty poor guys whose draft boards didn't even want them on account of some kind of health problem.

Yet instead of making everybody extra tense, the war loosened up a lot of rules. By the end of her first year, Bella belonged to a sort of club that never would have existed under ordinary conditions. It met, at odd moments, in a far corner of the law library—to play poker.

Bella considered herself an expert at this card game, but she may have been mistaken. As in any other contest, she played to win, grimly staying until the end of each deal even when she held nothing remotely like a winning combination. Such a system did have possibilities, because bluffing was an important tactic. However, if you were trying to fool your opponents into believing you had stronger cards than you really did, you had to keep a straight face—a poker face. That was a feat beyond Bella's power, for she could no more prevent her every feeling from flitting across her visage than she could stop breathing.

Fortunately, they played for very small stakes so she never lost much. And she really didn't play very often, because it was still no picnic to get the kind of marks Bella wanted. War or no war, a woman student had to work about twice as hard as a man did, just to prove that females weren't simple-minded, the way most of the professors assumed.

However, Bella positively would not follow the example of some of the other women students and put on a shy little girl performance. When it was her turn to present a test case, she hammered her points home instead of trying to charm the opposition, and if anybody got tough with her, she didn't just fold up, she got tough right back.

That definitely irritated some he-men who couldn't bear having a woman show them up. "What's a good-looking girl like you wasting her time for?" this type of fellow would say with a superior smirk. "You know you'll never practice law—you'll be too busy wheeling a baby carriage." Then there were even meaner ones who'd mutter, "Better watch out, Butch, or you'll get spanked."

While this kind of razzing didn't bother her too

much, and she did make plenty of friends, Bella sometimes wondered. Was she turning into some sort of freak? At least there was one person who didn't think so. Every couple of months Martin Abzug would turn up, legally or otherwise—she didn't know whether to believe him when he told her, peering clownishly to the left and right to see if anyone else was listening, that he'd snuck out of camp for the weekend because he couldn't live another day without feasting his eyes on her. Actually, she suspected that he had a pass safely tucked away in his wallet, and she more than suspected that she was getting somewhat fond of him. He really did look very handsome in his uniform. And who else would think of trying to impress her by giving her a magnificent set of books by the famous Supreme Court Justice Oliver Wendell Holmes for her birthday?

Of course, they fought almost constantly. "Bella, stop giving me a hard time!" he'd demand, but she'd go ahead anyway, telling him her opinion on whatever topic they were arguing about, usually something to do with their rather different ideas of the perfect future, once this terrible war was over. Martin thought it would be marvelous to buy a nice piece of scenic land in the country, and sit up on his hilltop writing novels. Ugh! Bella scoffed. How selfish could you be? With so much injustice crying out for correcting, any worthwhile person had to work on changing the system.

But whatever he said, Bella could tell that he

really admired her. When he was released from the army during her second year of law school, he proved it. Because he was fascinated by Broadway plays and movies, he wanted to go out practically every evening, though Bella couldn't possibly spare the time to accompany him. So he asked other dates; then after he took them home, he'd turn up at the law library toward midnight and see whether Bella had any notes ready for typing. If she did, he'd take them to his apartment—and deliver neatly typed papers to her on his next visit.

Yet it wasn't only his help in this department that Bella appreciated, nor his gift for making her laugh. Despite their many differences, they really did have a lot in common. They both loved music, swimming and—Bella finally admitted it—they loved each other.

So on the afternoon of June 4, 1944, a month before her twenty-fourth birthday, Bella Savitzky married Martin Abzug, who was now twenty-eight, while relatives from both of their families looked on with varying feelings. Bella's mother could hardly hold back her happy tears, but Martin's mother was not exactly overjoyed, though she did try to hide her disappointment. Since her husband's business had been prospering, she'd become very interested in money, and she thought her son should have chosen a rich wife. Besides, what kind of a life would he have if Bella insisted on working as a lawyer? Would they ever have children? Then when his mother at last accepted the fact that Martin's mind was made

Martin—and Law

up, she wanted to put on the wedding herself in some fancy hired hall, rather than be disgraced by a poor ceremony up in the Bronx.

Absolutely not, Bella said. She wouldn't have a fancy wedding under any circumstances, and with a war on she wouldn't even wear an expensive white dress. But thanks to Aunt Janet, she compromised. Uncle Julius had done as well as any Abzug, and Aunt Janet insisted that to uphold the honor of his sister's daughter, he would pay for a lovely party. Anyway, hadn't she practically introduced the young people to each other, and hadn't she been the first to recognize that here was a great match? By this time both of the young people were ready to sneak off to City Hall, but to please their families they gave in and spoke their vows at Aunt Janet's elegant apartment on Eastern Parkway in Brooklyn, with Bella wearing a lovely short dress of ice-blue silk and a matching hat.

Because of the undercurrent of tension between the two sets of relatives, Uncle Julius certainly had gone all out with his spending. A bar had been set up in the foyer, and except in a liquor store Martin had never seen as many bottles of whisky as were lined up there. With such prodigious supplies on hand, prodigious quantities of drinks were consumed. Soon Bella's other uncles were enthusiastically slapping Abzug backs. To make sure Martin realized how lucky he was, Uncle Hymie kept telling him Bella was "a diamond—a diamond!"

There was even more food than drink. Most of

Bella's uncles were in some branch of the meat business, so they were proud of knowing a good cut when they saw it, and they were also proud of their appetites. With the apartment's regular furniture temporarily moved, tables for a sit-down dinner were set in several rooms. No sooner had one table been served, than some uncle was hollering for more to eat. "What's the matter, Julius?" they shouted. "Are you running short? You getting stingy in your old age?"

Being accustomed to boisterous family parties, Bella had a fine time. But Martin was utterly bemused; he could not believe such enormous platters were being emptied so repeatedly. When all the relatives eventually got full, and departed, though the bar was still well-stocked only a few trays of little sandwiches were left for the couple's own friends, who'd been invited to a second installment of the celebration in the evening.

After they settled down, both bride and groom were even happier than either of them had anticipated. Because of the wartime shortage of apartments, the only quarters Martin could find for them was a small suite in a hotel on West Seventy-second Street. That suited Bella fine because it required practically no housekeeping chores, and it was just a short bus ride from Columbia, where she was in her third and last year of law school.

It was convenient for Martin, too, since he was working with his father about the same distance by bus in the other direction. But he didn't particularly enjoy being in the garment business, and this seemed a good time to find out whether he had the talent to be a writer as he'd always dreamed. So until Bella returned from her studying in the law library, he sat at his typewriter struggling to compose his first novel.

By the time Bella graduated from Columbia Law the following spring, he had several chapters she thought were pretty good. And Martin thought that what she had achieved was really terrific.

5

Three Lives

Looking back, Bella Abzug would sometimes feel that she lived three lives during the next several years—and enjoyed almost every minute of all of them.

Right after graduating from law school, then passing the New York State bar examination, she went to work at a law office specializing in labor union cases. Most of her classmates had sought jobs with stodgy old legal firms representing big business, but that sort of practice did not appeal to Bella. As far as she was concerned, making a lot of money was much less important than doing some good in this world.

And ever since President Roosevelt had fired her enthusiasm for his New Deal, she'd been a strong supporter of the union movement. During the war emergency, labor had patriotically put off most efforts to win better pay and working conditions. But the war had just ended!

So now there was a great surge to catch up, with the unions pressing for increased benefits, and management frequently striving to limit the influence of organized groups of employees rather than give them what they wanted. Here was a battle Bella could leap into wholeheartedly.

Her clients were mainly low-paid workers, and she poured prodigious energy into trying to help them. Most people would have been too tired out by the kind of schedule she routinely kept even to think of taking on any additional commitments. But if a Hunter friend called in tears because a landlord was refusing to provide any heat for aged and ailing parents, how could Bella just hang up?

So before long, she was running what amounted to a free legal advice bureau on her own time. And that was only part of her second life, for Bella could never turn down anybody who wanted her to join a committee or go to a meeting on behalf of a worthy cause. In fact, she thought everybody owed their community this kind of service. The idea that she deserved any special credit for doing so much extra, on top of her demanding job, never occurred to her.

It did occur to her husband, though, but instead of resenting his wife's busy schedule, he even encouraged her. If she was so fond of do-good activities, Martin would say cheerfully, that was fine with him. Being much less motivated along these lines himself, why shouldn't he be pleased to have her accomplishing enough for both of them?

Oh, sometimes it did irritate him if she rushed off to a meeting after dinner when he didn't feel like sitting at his typewriter. By now he'd finished *Seventh Avenue Story* and even sold it to a respected publisher, but he wasn't having as much fun with his second book, a novel about the war. He would have liked having her home more often, and yet the time they did spend together was so precious that he rarely complained.

For her part, Bella appreciated this third life with Martin more than she could express. While her work and her extra activities satisfied her craving to be a useful person, thanks to him she had a wonderful personal happiness she would otherwise have missed. It wasn't just that she would have been so lonely without his love, but also she would never have understood some of the deepest yearnings in every human being.

Back in college, she'd never thought much about having children. Of course, she loved kids, and she had a perfectly normal desire to have some of her own someday. But the way the system was set up, a man didn't have to sacrifice his whole career for the joy of being a father. Yet a woman was supposed to give up every other interest when she became a mother. Well, she didn't think that made sense, and so she'd more or less closed her mind to the plus aspects of motherhood.

Martin had tried to convince her, while they'd been arguing about whether to get married, that he'd be willing to go along with her continuing to work after they had a baby. They'd hire a housekeeper, he said. But who would stay home if the housekeeper got sick? Bella would throw up her hands and frown.

Yet after they did get married, it was Bella who got more and more anxious to have a baby. Beyond her emotional wish for one of life's great experiences, the stubborn part of her nature that made her hate to admit defeat also drove her in this direction because of some medical problems. Twice during the early years of their marriage, she had the thrill of being able to tell Martin she was pregnant, but then both times there were complications within the first few months and she suffered a miscarriage, ending the pregnancy. But instead of giving up after enduring so much pain and disappointment, she became more determined than ever.

Not that she didn't have other matters on her mind, too. In 1948, she and Martin were both ready to change their course professionally. He was fed up with the garment business, besides being convinced that he wasn't cut out to be a great novelist after all, so he was hoping to establish himself as a free-lance writer of magazine articles. As to Bella, she'd become so concerned about the way the civil rights of many Americans were being threatened that she wanted to open a law office of her own, concentrating on civil rights cases. While they were still discussing their plans, a grand opportunity presented itself.

Although she was only twenty-eight, the name of Bella Abzug had already become quite well known in the very small sector of the legal world where unpopular causes were willingly defended. So she decided to attend an international conference of lawyers on the subject of civil liberties. Since this conference was being held in Czechoslovakia, which had only recently come under Communist rule, anybody from the United States who participated ran the risk of being accused of having Communist sympathies—a serious charge, with anti-Red feeling running high among people who proudly labeled themselves as "one hundred per cent Americans." But Bella had always hated the practice of giving people labels, even if she'd willingly admit supporting many leftist causes, and she jumped at this chance to go to Europe.

So did Martin. For they decided it was a good time to take a long trip, exploring countries they might not ever get to visit after they both settled into new occupations.

England. France. Switzerland. They traveled all over those lands, seeing the famous cities and quaint towns, besides swimming wherever they found a beach and hiking up and down steep mountain paths, before they finally arrived in Prague, the beautiful old capital of Czechoslovakia. Here Bella enjoyed talking with the leading figures in her chosen field.

But a few days later she was flat on her back in a hotel room, and a doctor who spoke hardly any English was trying to give her some advice. For she was pregnant again, with symptoms that might mean another miscarriage. No! Bella would not let herself think of the possibility.

They were now in Poland, on their way to look for the village where Martin's family had originally lived. Finding this place had been a dream of his, so Bella insisted that he go on without her, and at last he did. By the time he returned, she really was feeling much better.

Several months later, safely back in New York, Bella gave birth to a daughter they named Eve Gail —Egee, they called her, liking the sound of her initials. Martin had found them an apartment on Central Park West, where his wife's friends flocked to see her grin as she carefully picked up her own little baby.

Yet much as she relished her new role of being a mother, Bella never for an instant considered giving up her law work. They were fortunate enough to hear about a warm-hearted woman who wanted a housekeeping job, and with Alice Williams watching Egee, there was nothing to worry about on that score. But there was a whole lot else to worry about, with Senator Joseph McCarthy of Wisconsin leading a vicious campaign to persecute anybody he suspected of Communist leanings.

So Bella Abzug did open her own law office, and

soon a stream of frightened people was keeping her busier than ever. Most of them had no particular claim to fame—they were schoolteachers or clerks or practically unknown radio actors, fired from their jobs merely because somebody accused them of being "un-American." For in the hysteria fanned by McCarthyism, it had suddenly become a crime to join not only the Communist party, but also a long list of so-called "subversive" organizations. Even to be named by some anonymous informer meant instant disgrace.

What about freedom of speech? Lawyer Abzug would scornfully ask the question in court. Since when was it un-American to criticize the government, or to try to change some unfair law that badly needed changing? What about Patrick Henry and Thomas Jefferson? Weren't the forces striving to stifle free speech in the 1950s the real threat to American democracy?

Her voice throbbing with passion, Bella won some cases and her clients got their jobs back. But whether she won or lost, there were no headlines about the verdict. Because her clients were just ordinary citizens, hardly anybody paid any attention to their victories or defeats. Then, in 1951, she took on the defense of a thirty-two-year-old truck driver from a small town down South, charged with a different crime—and that case made headlines all around the world.

Willie McGee, a black man who'd lived all his life

Lawyer Abzug confers with a client at a 1955 hearing of the House Un-American Activities Committee investigating alleged Communist ties among New York theater people. *United Press International photo*

in Mississippi, had already been condemned to death for raping a white woman when some militant civil rights activists sought help on appealing the sentence. But soon after his arrest, he'd confessed he was guilty, so on what grounds could he be saved?

When Bella studied the record, she was immediately struck by several points. Though McGee had admitted having sexual relations with his accuser, he'd said she willingly made love on many occasions over a three-year period, and had only protested about being attacked after her husband discovered a black man in her bedroom. Of course, she'd protested to save her own skin, Bella swiftly decided. For in the Deep South then, a white woman who voluntarily had any intimate relationship with a black man was breaking a law, besides violating the most fiercely enforced restriction in the whole fabric of racial prejudice. A husband would be congratulated by the white community for getting rid of such a wife; he'd probably be excused even for killing her. Why wouldn't a white woman lie about who was at fault if she was caught with a black man?

In fact she was expected to lie, Bella grimly noted. Then the black man could be punished, teaching others like him the basic lesson that they'd better not ever touch any white female. Until all too recently this lesson had been taught at the end of a rope, with lynch mobs taking the law into their own hands. Yet wasn't the law still acting with no more fairness than a lynching party? How often was a white man executed for the crime of rape?

It just didn't happen, Bella knew even without searching in any law books. Nevertheless, she spent weeks studying the verdicts in sex cases handed

Three Lives

down by Mississippi juries, and when she was finished she had page after page of documentation that struck her as clear proof for a new sort of defense. From the moment Willie McGee had been arrested, throughout his trial and in his sentencing to death, this man had repeatedly been treated differently from any white defendant, solely because his skin was black.

While Bella had been doing her research, other concerned people had been busy too. A campaign to send letters and telegrams to Mississippi's governor, demanding fair treatment for Willie McGee, brought forth a stream of mail, not only from many parts of the United States but also from a number of foreign countries. This infuriated a lot of white Southerners who felt "outsiders" had no right to interfere. The fact that some of the protests came from the Soviet Union and Red China further inflamed the issue, because it convinced some people that the whole effort to save McGee must be a Communist plot.

By the beginning of May, when the appeal for a pardon was scheduled to be heard in Mississippi's capital of Jackson, Bella was in the early stages of a new pregnancy. She knew that Martin wished she had not gotten involved with this case right now, because public opinion in Jackson was turning ugly, and she might even be subjected to physical violence there. Any lawyer from the North would be a target for abuse, and the fact that she was a woman would make her more unpopular since she was ignoring the unwritten law forbidding a white woman to speak up for a black man accused of such a crime. Furthermore, that she was Jewish would give the bigots of the community added grounds for hating her.

But Martin made no move to keep her from departing. "Nobody's got Bella's guts," he proudly told their friends, and she remembered his words when she got off a bus to find that no hotel in town would let her have a room. A taxi driver suggested that they could try a motel fifteen miles away. She didn't like that idea though.

So she sat up all night in the bus station, just barely managing to doze off a few minutes before it was time to wash her face in the ladies' room, then walk to the capitol grounds where dozens of protesters were already marching.

Despite her lack of sleep, she pleaded for six hours to the special board appointed by the governor, begging them to pardon Willie McGee. She insisted that McGee had been the victim of a conspiracy on the part of Mississippi officials—a conspiracy to violate his civil rights because of racial prejudice—and she listed instance after instance of unfair treatment during his trial and earlier appeals. By canceling his death sentence, she said, they would immeasurably strengthen faith in American democracy everywhere.

Although she had won two previous delays, she failed in this final appeal, as she had feared she would. On the front page of *The New York Times* the next morning, there was a headline she cried as she read:

WILLIE M'GEE GOES TO ELECTRIC CHAIR

In the last paragraph of the long article reporting on the execution, and on the protest marchers and other efforts to save a black man who had become a symbol of oppression, her own name was mentioned for the first time, although her arguments had been summarized in several previous paragraphs. "McGee's attorneys," the writer noted, "were John Coe of Pensacola, Fla., and Mrs. Bella Abzug of New York City, an attractive 30-year-old lawyer." Well, someday she would show them she was more than attractive.

6

Mount Vernon

Bella's second daughter—Isobel Jo, but they called her Liz—was born in 1952, and soon it became obvious that the family would have to move again. Not even a larger apartment would solve the problem, Martin kept telling his wife, for children needed the fresh air and freedom of the country to grow up healthy and happy.

Was that so? Bella grumbled a little about how she and her husband had both survived as city kids, along with countless others, but she really could not object seriously to any plan supposed to benefit the babies. Also, she had to admit that the upper Bronx in her day differed quite a bit from crowded Manhattan these days. All right, let them go where the girls would thrive, and yet couldn't it be no more than a half-hour ride from her office?

It could. For Martin's mother was willing to sell them her house in the suburb of Mount Vernon, linked to the city by fast and frequent train service. There were a lot of suburbs where they wouldn't have wanted to live, but one of the best features of Mount Vernon, as far as they were concerned, was the fact that their new neighbors included several black families, so their girls would attend an integrated school and wouldn't be exposed to the racially prejudiced atmosphere of many other suburban communities.

However, the true picture turned out to be less peaceful than they'd been led to expect. After they moved, it didn't take them long to discover that some real estate operators were doing all they could to stir up trouble. On any block with a few black families, white homeowners were being urged to sell out fast, before the neighborhood became mainly black and the value of their house dropped sharply. Of course, the real estate people hoped to make a quick profit for themselves by spreading fear this way, and they really didn't care about what such "block-busting" tactics usually accomplished.

But Bella Abzug did. As if she didn't have enough else to do, she began to organize a committee of neighbors to fight the block-busters. We've got a good area here for our kids and for all of us, she kept saying, and we can keep it from changing—unless we panic. Whether the neighbors were black or white, most of them were impressed when Bella ridiculed the idea that they were powerless to prevent their street from becoming part of a black ghetto. Powerless? Why, if they'd just slam the door on any sly character out to scare them, they could stop this whole thing cold!

Wasn't it true, though, that more and more black customers were coming around to look at local houses? Sure it was, Bella said, but they weren't coming by themselves; they were being lured by the block-busters who didn't care a bit about the problems blacks had in finding a decent place to live. The aim of the game was to trick blacks into paying a high price for a house in an integrated community, meanwhile tipping the racial balance further and further toward the all-black direction. Then, when the figure passed a certain point, banks would refuse to lend any money to improve or even to keep up the property in such an "undesirable" neighborhood, and sooner or later the whole area probably would turn into a slum. But who said this had to happen?

Several evenings a week, month after month, Bella hammered away at various plans for thwarting the block-busters. Special efforts were started to attract white families who didn't want to bring up their children in a white-only environment. Groups of neighbors agreed that even if they did have to move away for some good reason and were putting their homes up for sale, they wouldn't do any business with real estate agents playing the block-busting game. But every so often somebody would say it couldn't work, they'd all better sell while they could, and nasty rumors would start flying again.

Although Bella might get discouraged briefly, she'd always bounce back in a day or two. For she had so many different things going on at the same time that she was almost bound to cheer up as a new challenge confronted her. Instead of just the three lives she'd lived during the first years of her marriage, now she had four.

In the city, she still had her law work, plus her extra activities. In the suburbs, besides her family she also had a whole new category of projects such as her campaign against the block-busters. Yet somehow she managed to keep juggling them all, over a period of nearly fifteen years. "It was pretty tough," she would recall later with a slight smile.

Of course, it wouldn't have been possible without Martin's help. His free-lance writing on economic subjects had led to a job in the Wall Street area, selling stocks and bonds. Though he was commuting, too, back and forth between Mount Vernon and Manhattan five days a week, he had a more predictable schedule than his wife did, so he could be home well before dinner every evening to play games with the girls while they were small, to hear their latest news from school as they got older. When Bella was delayed at her office, or had a night meeting in the city, she'd feel relieved that at least one parent would be keeping the girls company.

Thanks to Alice Williams, who'd willingly moved up from the city with them, Egee and Liz got plenty of attention even if both parents were busy elsewhere. Alice loved and soothed the children through all sorts of minor troubles, and she liked to tell Bella, "I all but had those kids." Sometimes their mother couldn't avoid a qualm of guilt about not being with her daughters enough herself, but then she would look at other mothers who did nothing but hover over their children, and think that maybe Egee and Liz weren't so badly off after all. For they'd learned right from the cradle that a mother could have important work to do out in the world. So they'd never be oppressed themselves by any old-fashioned ideas that a woman wasn't supposed to be a doctor or a lawyer or whatever else she wanted to aim for.

Not that Bella put her legal work ahead of motherhood on her personal scale of values. Particularly as the girls grew bigger, she tried hard to get home for dinner with them every evening and to keep up with all of their interests. If one of them was in a school play, she'd take a day off to see it. Because she was anxious for them to have a sound religious training, she sent them to a Jewish cultural school cooperatively run by a group of parents.

Then every summer she'd escape for a full month from her jangling office telephone, and have a marvelous time on the beach with Martin and the kids. To make sure she wouldn't be interrupted, they'd rent an island cottage where no calls could reach her.

Even so, when she looked back after her daughters were grown up, she might find herself wishing that she had given a larger share of her energy to being a mother. "I should have been more available," she would tell herself. Almost immediately, though, she would have to shrug and ask what she could have done differently. Which law cases could she have turned down, which causes could she have failed to support? It just wasn't easy to be a lawyer and a mother and a concerned citizen all at the same time.

Mainly because she was a mother, though, she made one of the most important decisions of her career early in 1960. She was sitting around with several other lawyers, talking about the latest series of nuclear bomb tests by the Soviet Union and the United States. During the preceding months, scientists in many countries had been voicing increasingly sharp warnings about the dangerous fallout from such explosions. Practically all over the world, there were reports that the air and water now held alarming amounts of radioactive substances. Cows grazing on grass that seemed perfectly harmless were giving milk with definite traces of the terrible strontium 90, capable of causing cancer.

Bella Abzug had heard all of this before, and yet it had never impressed her as it did that day. What if Egee and Liz were still babies! Or maybe they'd have children of their own eventually. Were millions of infants to be condemned to a horrible death because so-called statesmen would not stop these awful tests?

Suddenly Bella looked stunned.

"There was an explosion in my mind," she explained later. Until that instant, she had considered herself a successful lawyer with at least a normal amount of personal ambition. In her line of work, one of the highest aims was to win an appeal before the Supreme Court, but now she heard herself saying, "I don't care if I win a case in the Supreme Court. I'm going to worry about the world."

Sure, she had done her share of worrying all along, and maybe she'd scattered her shots too much? No more, though. While she wouldn't exactly close her own office and give up everything else, from now on what she was going to do was to concentrate on the most urgent issue facing the whole human race—the issue of stopping the dreadful atomic tests.

But Bella made very little headway at first. Most of her fellow citizens appeared to be more interested in their private concerns than in the state of the world. President Eisenhower's warm smile reassured them that the nation's affairs were being sensibly managed, and anybody who dared to criticize American policies was widely assumed to be some sort of crank, if not an outright traitor trying to help the Soviet Union overtake the United States in military power.

Nevertheless, there were some Americans with a deep sense of shame about the way their country was competing in the nuclear arms race, and many thousands of people overseas, from Japan to Sweden, were protesting vigorously. In England, every Easter week increasing numbers of young people and old, factory workers and famous scientists, were stopping

Mount Vernon

London traffic with a huge "Ban the Bomb" parade. It was a London demonstration in 1961 that sent a spark across the Atlantic, finally inflaming the fire Bella Abzug had been trying to start.

For Bertrand Russell, a world-renowned mathematics professor and philosopher who was approaching his ninetieth birthday, had been arrested during the course of this protest. Despite his great age, he had joined a militant group bent on disobeying police orders to call attention to the peace movement, and as a result he was locked up in a London jail. The following day, not very far from the White House, a woman with three daughters and a modest reputation as an illustrator of children's books—ordinarily a calm person, not particularly interested in politics—was sitting in her own garden reading a newspaper when she came upon the story about Bertrand Russell.

"It made me so mad I wanted to hire a jet and go over there and picket the jail," Dagmar Wilson told an interviewer several weeks later. The reason this usually shy and unassuming woman was being interviewed was that, instead of just simmering down, Mrs. Wilson had picked up her phone and called a few friends to see if they felt the same way she did.

Indeed they did. They all shared her outrage at the imprisonment of a famous old man who was speaking out for the sake of all humanity. So that evening six women gathered in the Wilson living room. From that small meeting came one of the most remarkable

Some of Bella's supporters waiting to board a train for Washington with her. *Sheldon Ramsdell photo*

crusades in American history—the Women Strike for Peace.

For each of those six women called friends in other cities, and soon there were several hundred women busy on their telephones. Without any political experience or any headquarters, they planned to express their feelings about the nuclear arms race by holding a series of protest marches on November first. But how could such an amateur effort create the

Mount Vernon

slightest ripple? Newspaper and TV news editors thought they were probably wasting a lot of effort when they assigned reporters to the story.

They were mistaken.

On November 1, 1961, several thousand women marched up and down the sidewalk outside the White House, carrying peace signs. There were grandmothers and college students, and many young mothers wheeling their infants in strollers. For the benefit of cameramen, toddlers held up posters asking President Kennedy, who had been elected just the year before, to make sure their milk was safe.

Nothing like this mass demonstration of women had been seen in Washington since the suffrage marches half a century earlier, when America's women were demanding the right to vote. But peace marchers also turned out in fifty-eight other cities all across the country. Were there fifty thousand altogether? Or twice that number? Nobody really knew.

One of the largest assemblages was on First Avenue in New York City, directly opposite the gleaming new headquarters of the United Nations. Among this crowd of marching women, it was easy to pick out Bella Abzug. "Peace!" she was shouting, as she happily waved new arrivals into the parade.

For the time had finally come when Bella was no longer almost alone in her urge to do something about stopping atomic testing. The leaders of this new women's movement, appealing for the support of women everywhere, had even written to Mrs. John

F. Kennedy and to Mrs. Nikita Khrushchev, asking them to try to influence their husbands to "end the arms race, not the human race." Though Bella hadn't thought up this great crusade herself, it struck her as a marvelous idea—and soon she was deeply involved in helping to direct it.

Originally, Dagmar Wilson and her friends hadn't any notion of doing more than staging a one-day protest, but the national response they stirred was tremendously encouraging. In the next several months, informal chapters began operation wherever there were some women willing to devote their time and effort to the cause. Although Bella Abzug definitely fit into this category, she didn't believe she could accomplish nearly as much in Mount Vernon as she could in New York City. And that's where she began organizing.

By now Egee was twelve and Liz nine, and their mother was starting to wonder how much longer she'd have to endure commuting. Until they finished high school, Martin said, and Bella didn't feel she could argue this point. She'd stood nearly ten years of train riding already; somehow she'd get through another eight or nine.

But as Bella got busier and busier with the peace committees she was trying to put together downtown, she began noticing a strange fact. Almost every Saturday when she was taking off for a meeting, Egee wanted to come along to the city and go to a museum or some art show. Art was her big interest;

Mount Vernon

she was talking about becoming a sculptor. At last it occurred to Bella to ask her older daughter a simple question. Would she by any chance like the idea of moving back to Manhattan?

Would she!

It still took a few years to convince Martin, who kept asking what about the little one? But Liz had a lovely singing voice, and the chances were that she'd major in music when she got to high school. At New York's famous High School of Music and Art, she could certainly do that better than in Mount Vernon. So in 1965, at least four years sooner than Bella had dared to hope, the family packed up to leave the suburbs.

While Bella was not sorry to be departing, she did have to admit that these thirteen years had been quite an experience. Even if the block-busters hadn't exactly won, they had not lost, either, and the neighborhood was still being threatened with downgrading by the zoning board. But Martin had found someone willing to take a chance on Mount Vernon's future, who had friends anxious to raise the money to help her get a new start in the country. He sold their house to the widow of Malcolm X, and the Abzugs moved to Greenwich Village.

7

From Peace to Politics

Their new home was the lower two floors of a handsome old house on a narrow street that hadn't changed much in at least a hundred years. There were trees along the curb, and clusters of ivy climbing up the red brick walls. Around the corner, little food markets and shops displaying the latest in belts or books or jewelry stayed open late, while neon signs flickered outside all sorts of restaurants. Here the sidewalks were thronged with some of the city's most interesting-looking people, and with tourists hoping to see a real live artist or hippie.

For Greenwich Village was New York's version of the Left Bank in Paris and the Haight-Ashbury district of San Francisco. But besides being a magnet for artists and the "flower children" of the era, the

From Peace to Politics

Village also housed numerous well-off families who enjoyed its special flavor and the fact that it was so close to the midtown area.

Bella Abzug felt they couldn't have made a better move. Both girls seemed happy at their new schools, Martin was happy to be about ten minutes from his office, and she herself was positively elated by the whole urban scene. Of course, they were lucky to be able to afford such a comfortable place just a short walk from the subway, combining the best features of city and suburban living as far as she was concerned. They had plenty of space to spread out in, yet they could get wherever they wanted to go in practically no time flat.

And Bella certainly did keep on the go, with new peace groups springing up all over the city now. Two years before, back in 1963, a limited nuclear test ban treaty signed by the United States, the Soviet Union, and Great Britain had given the movement its first taste of victory. This treaty outlawed the testing of hydrogen bombs in the atmosphere. But underground testing was still allowed. Furthermore, only the three nations that had signed the agreement were bound by its terms, so what would happen as other countries inevitably developed a nuclear capability? And how could there be any real hope for the future while the world's major powers were still spending billions in their every budget on long-range missiles, besides countless other terrifying weapons?

Until this insane arms race was halted, there would

be a desperate need for continued protest, according to Bella and an increasing number of other people. Even more urgently, they felt that America's mounting intervention in Vietnam violated the basic principles of international law, in addition to being a disgraceful waste of this nation's resources. To make the United Sates change its policy toward Vietnam was becoming the main aim of the peace movement, with Bella Abzug becoming more and more involved in its New York campaign.

Somehow the word got around, east side and west, uptown and down, that anybody who wanted to join the movement should contact her. "There's this peace woman," one person told another. "She'll help you organize."

They were mainly housewives, the women who got in touch with her. Nice women, intelligent and well educated, but Bella was well aware that only a few years before, some of them would have been barely polite to her. For it hadn't been considered respectable then to challenge your country's foreign policy: only Communist sympathizers would dream of arguing with the Pentagon officials who said that America's security depended on spending billions for weapons—or so these nice women had been taught. Someone like Bella Abzug, who'd never made any secret of her leftist political leaning, would almost automatically have been called a Communist. What a relief, Bella would murmur every so often, that being for peace had now become respectable.

From Peace to Politics

Yet she didn't mean to poke fun at her new allies. She welcomed them all, knowing full well that it still wasn't easy for them to challenge the prevailing public opinion. After every peace march, ridiculous letters to the editor would appear in newspapers, written by men smugly telling "the ladies" they ought to leave matters they could not understand to their superior menfolk. Even more infuriating were the women who wrote to say they didn't want their children drinking contaminated milk either, but the right way to work for peace was to stand firmly behind our elected leaders because, naturally, they knew more than any woman could about how to preserve and protect American democracy.

Naturally? When Bella read this kind of lamebrained nittering, she thanked heaven that at least some women had finally learned to think for themselves. The Women Strike for Peace! The very name of their movement excited her, with its ringing sound of action. She liked that much better than the Women's Strike, which was the way most newspapers insisted on referring to it. Whatever you called it, though, she couldn't help realizing that this magnificent effort owed its existence to the aroused conscience of a small portion of the population.

But working-class women ought to be marching, too. And working men, the whole labor movement, not to mention youth groups as well as senior citizens, black groups and all sorts of ethnic groups—every sort of group anybody could think of, for wasn't everybody deeply affected by the nation's growing commitment to this atrocious war in Asia?

Bella's voice would drip with scorn as she talked about the "advisers" the United States had sent over to Vietnam, instead of letting both sides in what was really a civil war settle their affairs their own way. But now we were even sending American soldiers to fight battles that were none of their business. American boys were being drafted to go there, some of them were dying, and American planes were dropping bombs, killing innocent people, burning up villages, destroying a beautiful country.

What's more, all this evil was costing billions that even the rich United States could not spare, Bella would insist. Look at our own city, she'd say, with its awful slums and its welfare mess, its polluted air and its drug epidemic; the city was falling to pieces because so much money was being drained off to pay the immense bills that the Pentagon kept handing to President Johnson.

At first Bella did most of her speaking at small meetings in other people's living rooms, but by 1967 she was finding larger audiences because her idea of broadening the base of the peace movement was bearing fruit. Now there were peace action committees working in many neighborhoods, trying to enlist the support of every segment of the community. Rallies and demonstrations were bringing out more and more concerned citizens.

Yet what could they hope to accomplish? Ever

From Peace to Politics

since the end of World War II, there had been a few committees of people who risked being called kooks or Communist dupes to try to influence government policies, with practically no success. True enough, said Bella, but the situation had changed, and she was going to see that it changed a whole lot more in the months to come.

For Bella Abzug was now making regular trips to Washington.

There was still only a loose sort of organization uniting the hundreds of chapters of the Women Strike for Peace. It had no funds to pay a staff, but if WSP were to have any real impact, it needed a political action director and a legislative director. Both of these jobs could be lumped together under the less formal title of chief lobbyist, and on a volunteer basis that's what Bella had become.

She was leading one delegation after another to tell members of Congress how a lot of New Yorkers felt about Vietnam. Not only the Representatives from city districts, but also most of the powerful figures in both houses grew accustomed to the sight of a purposeful woman striding toward them with a group of supporters in her wake.

"Here comes the mothers' lobby," a staff aide would mutter, and many of the members would try to hide. Even those who didn't like what was happening in Vietnam themselves would often keep Bella and her group waiting for hours in the anterooms of their offices.

So we're not worth talking to, Bella would say angrily. What kind of nonsense was this? But gradually, as the peace movement gained momentum and huge demonstrations were held in several cities, more doors were opened to them. Still Bella wasn't satisfied. Why should they always be on the outside, begging their elected lawmakers to listen to them? Why didn't they have some of their own people on the inside, actually helping to make decent laws and putting American democracy back on the right track?

The same thought struck more than a few other women in the peace movement. And they had another question, addressed to Bella herself.

"Why don't *you* run?"

Bella didn't even pretend to be surprised. Of course she had thought vaguely about running for office; she'd thought of it a long time ago, she would freely admit. But there was a limit to what a woman could try to do; she didn't like to say so and yet she couldn't deny it, she told some of her friends with a rueful smile. In the kind of society we had in the United States, a woman who had children would be making life extremely difficult for her family if she put on a real campaign to win a seat in Congress, let alone if she managed to get elected.

Sure, Martin had been wonderful all these years about taking over a larger share of domestic duties than most men would. He didn't have any feeling that his manhood was being threatened when he carried home a bag of groceries. But it simply wouldn't be fair to expect him to assume the whole responsibility for their very lively household, any more than it would be fair if he expected her to do the whole job herself.

With two teen-age daughters, lively was the right word, Bella would add cheerfully. They were great girls, they really were, but it wasn't easy to grow up these days when so many old ideas had been tossed out the window and some of the new ones were just terrible, like all this drug business. Bella, being such a natural rebel, felt a lot of sympathy for all these young people doing their own thing—by all means, let them wear blue jeans if it made them happy and cut their hair however they wanted to, or not at all. Still, she hated to hear of any kid risking severe health problems from going on drug trips, which thankfully didn't seem to interest either of her girls.

Not that they both didn't have their problems, but that was only to be expected. Egee, like a lot of other older sisters, took things pretty seriously sometimes, maybe because parents tended to be a bit tense with their first babies, yet she had a marvelous sense of humor and Bella was sure she'd make a success at whatever she finally settled on doing. Despite her talent for sculpturing, Egee now wanted to major in philosophy when she went to college the coming September.

Yes, their older one would be leaving the nest very soon, although she'd just be flying as far as Hofstra out on Long Island. But the little one, which was the way Bella couldn't help referring to Liz, would still have three more years at home, commuting by subway to the High School of Music and Art uptown. Wouldn't you know, this lighthearted kid with such a beautiful singing voice was saying she'd really like to be a lawyer! Bella wouldn't try to stop her—that wasn't her style—but in the next three years she'd have to make a point of being available while Liz was going through the never easy passage from fifteen to eighteen.

After that—Bella would shrug, and try to look mystified—after that, who could tell? Maybe she would decide to take the plunge into politics herself, but meanwhile she'd have to stay on the outside, merely expressing her opinions to various elected representatives.

However, she carried this process well beyond the usual range of lobbying activities. As the presidential election of 1968 approached, the peace movement was becoming a political force that could no longer be ignored on the grounds that it spoke for only a small minority of impractical idealists. Borrowing the tactics of old-fashioned backroom bosses, some of its leaders set up a calculated plan to accomplish a rare feat in American political history—to prevent an incumbent President from winning his party's nomination for another term. "Dump Johnson" was their slogan, and Bella Abzug endorsed it enthusiastically.

She spent the early months of 1968 trying to

From Peace to Politics

arouse a commitment in this direction among the district leaders of Manhattan's Democrats. Then when Lyndon Johnson announced at the end of March that, to promote party unity, he would not be a candidate in November, Bella worked even harder to build widespread support for an anti-war stand by the national convention of the Democratic party, scheduled to convene that August in Chicago.

To get a peace candidate and a peace platform, Bella kept saying, it was absolutely essential to have unified action by many different groups. A coalition was needed, she insisted, a combined effort on the part of peace groups, women's groups, poor people, black and other minorities, by every segment of the population that had not been adequately represented until now and that was finally ready to demand an end to the United States involvement in Vietnam.

When August arrived, thousands of peace marchers gathered outside the convention hall in Chicago, and there were also official delegates inside who were pledged to vote for peace. Though they were not a majority, it seemed reasonable to expect that many uncommitted delegates would be swayed by the mass demonstrations in the streets and would join the peace contingent.

However, reason had no chance to prevail in Chicago that year. For the city's police and the peace marchers clashed in a terrifying outbreak of rioting, which Bella and her friends blamed almost completely on the club-swinging police tactics encouraged by the inner circle of party leaders. Sure, some of the kids might have been hard to control—and if they did get a little rough, it was easy to understand why, although Bella didn't believe violence ever solved anything. Yet nothing they did could possibly excuse the orgy of head-smashing the so-called protectors of law and order proceeded to indulge in, while the convention shamefully droned on just as if there were no blood staining the downtown area of the nation's second largest city.

But this terrible spectacle was seen everywhere on television, and no matter who was to blame, even Bella realized that the peace movement had suffered a severe blow. So had the Democratic party itself, which now seemed too divided to be able to govern the country effectively. Vice President Hubert Humphrey had won the party's nomination for the nation's highest office, and he tried during his campaign to convince the peace wing that he was moving toward their position, at the same time also striving to reassure voters of every shade of opinion that he could be trusted in the White House.

Instead, the nation put its trust in the Republican candidate, Richard Nixon. Eight years earlier, running against John F. Kennedy in 1960, he'd lost in the closest election on record, at least partly because a lot of people thought a little joke that kept popping up all over the country was more than funny. Somebody would clip a solemn portrait of Nixon out of a newspaper and pass it around with the deadpan com-

From Peace to Politics

ment: "Would you buy a used car from this man?" But if Nixon's long record in politics had made many of his fellow citizens mildly suspect him of not always telling the truth, Bella Abzug was not a bit mild in her opinion of him. She hated him.

For she had a long memory about political dirty tricks, and she remembered very clearly back in 1950 when Congressman Richard Nixon of California had decided he wanted to be a United States Senator. His opponent in that campaign was a capable and lovely woman named Helen Gahagan Douglas, who'd already served several years in Congress. She was a New Deal Democrat whose loyalty to American democracy could not be doubted, but that did not stop Nixon. He attacked her so bitterly for being "soft on Communism," using what turned out later to be faked or misleading documents to bolster his charges, that he not only won the election, but he also drove a fine person out of politics.

Possibly Bella Abzug had been influenced even more than she thought by the sad case of Mrs. Douglas. Here was a woman who'd been defeated in public life by a man who had no scruples about distorting facts, and she'd been too crushed to fight back effectively. Well, it was one thing to have sensitive feelings but quite another to let a bully assume that any female would just fade away if her feelings were hurt. In her law practice, Bella had been insulted often enough by sarcastic men. No matter how she felt inside, though, she'd never backed away

Bella marching in a St. Patrick's Day parade on Fifth Avenue in New York shortly after she entered politics. *Jean Wolcott photo*

from a fight. And if she got into politics she certainly would go right on fighting whenever it was necessary.

If! Who was she kidding? With that evil man in the White House, she surely would run for Congress at the very next election.

So even before Liz finished high school, during her

second daughter's senior year Bella began letting friends know she'd be needing some help very soon. From her own high school days and from Hunter, from every stage in her career, Bella had acquired dozens of friends who heard her news early in 1970.

Mim Kelber, who'd been at both Walton and Hunter with Bella, and who'd done most of the writing for WSP while Bella had been doing most of the lobbying, was not exactly surprised by Bella's latest plan. But even Bella couldn't challenge the party machine in her election district without hundreds of people to help her. It would be a huge job to get signatures on petitions just to start with, and Bella had no organization. Whom could she call on?

The question seemed to amuse Bella, for her lips twitched into a smile that quickly changed into the broadest possible grin. Without a word, she waved both arms in the "Come-on-and-follow-me!" gesture she was always using when she shepherded hundreds of women into another march for peace—and Mim burst out laughing.

Of course! Now they'd be ringing doorbells for Bella. But couldn't she think of a better campaign slogan than that?

8

"This Woman's Place..."

In the spring of 1970, posters blossomed up and down the west side of Manhattan. They showed a smiling Bella, with the slogan she had chosen: "This woman's place is in the House—the House of Representatives."

But her first order of business was to capture control of the Democratic party right in her own district, and that wouldn't be easy. Congressman Leonard Farbstein, who had already served seven terms, would certainly not step aside just because somebody else wanted to replace him. Bella would have to win a primary contest in June before she could even get onto the ballot for the regular November election.

This primary would be terribly important, for Bella knew that as a political newcomer she stood no chance of getting sent to Washington without the endorsement of a major party. Even if it didn't happen to be true that Democrats usually won elections in her district, she naturally would seek the Democratic nomination because she'd been a Democrat since Franklin D. Roosevelt's day. But the so-called reform wing of the party, to which she belonged, had tried repeatedly to defeat Farbstein, never succeeding, and some of her friends warned her about what a hard job she was undertaking. Nevertheless, other friends encouraged her. "He's like a piece of furniture," they told her. "It's time he was moved."

While Bella didn't particularly enjoy moving furniture, here was a task she relished. So she spent sixteen hours most days in May walking the crowded streets of Manhattan, grabbing the hands of total strangers.

"Hi!" she'd greet them, "I'm Bella Abzug." Then she'd proceed to tell them with great enthusiasm why she'd do better at representing them in Congress than Farbstein had been doing. "I'm the kind of person who *does* things," she'd say, proving her point by the vigor of her handshake. "I'm down to earth," she'd add, and the sound of a real New Yorker in her hoarse voice would make that clear. She even approached construction workers with their hard hats, who were supposed to be strong supporters of President Nixon's policy in Vietnam. While they sat on steel girders eating their lunch, she shouted up at them that this war was hurting the economy, there'd be fewer buildings being built if it didn't get stopped, which was just what she aimed to fight for.

"You tell 'em, Bella!" a taxi driver would holler out of his cab window.

But all the political experts remembered that Farbstein had beaten every previous challenger. Although he might not be much of a speaker, he, too, opposed the war in Vietnam, he favored better housing, his moderately liberal opinions reflected the prevailing views of his district, so why should he have any trouble winning again?

Yet he did.

On the night of June 23, when the primary votes were counted, it turned out that the 19th Congressional District had a new Democratic candidate. By the small but safe margin of about 2,500, Bella Abzug had scored a victory none of the experts had expected.

Then suddenly the media "discovered" her. That Saturday, a full page in the *New York Post* was captioned:

WOMAN IN THE NEWS: BELLA ABZUG
A "Hellraiser" Heads
for Congress

Even the *Washington Post* devoted half a page on Sunday to a feature story with the headline:

LOWER MANHATTAN'S BELLA ABZUG
RASPS IT LIKE IT IS.

While Bella knew perfectly well that she had to put up with being interviewed—because she still had a fight for election facing her in the fall and the publicity might help her to beat her Republican opponent—she could hardly read a lot of what they wrote about her. "Battling Bella," they called her, and all sorts of other silly titles. They made fun of her voice, going so far as to compare it with a foghorn; they acted as if the way she looked were more important than what she stood for by composing a first paragraph like, "A startled advertising executive said, 'I thought she was a truck driver; she scared the hell out of me.'"

If she were a man, she fumed, nobody would write this kind of drivel.

Yet, many of her friends urged her to calm down and consider the political realities. In New York City, there simply was no such thing as a safe district that would always choose its candidates by their party label. Most voters liked to brag about how independent they were, and about how they made up their minds on the basis of the individual candidate rather than party loyalty. But even if professors of political science hated to admit it, a lot of people found politics pretty boring. So anybody with Bella Abzug's gift for making politics interesting had an advantage that might swing an election. Let the newspapers do their worst; the more of a character they made her out to be, the more they helped her.

Then Bella's lips would purse in her private little

smile. As if she had to be told that people would rather vote for a real person than for a stock politician!

Not that the man she was running against could be dismissed so lightly. On the contrary, Republican Barry Farber was the host of a local radio talk show, and he had quite a following. Furthermore, the primary battle she'd narrowly won had left bitter feelings among some old-time Democrats. Just out of spite, they were talking about supporting her opponent in November.

By winning the primary, Bella had automatically become the favorite as far as the experts were concerned. But instead of relaxing during the summer, she put on a campaign that made the whole country sit up and take notice.

In the first place, she commanded attention like a star performer facing an audience. "What am I doing here?" she would ask at a Chinatown meeting, then shrug her shoulders and pause while she pondered her own question. "I'm a fifty-year-old woman, an established lawyer, a wife, and mother of two daughters." Again she would pause, looking very solemn. "Believe me," she demanded, "the last thing I need at this point in my life is to knock my brains out to get elected to Congress."

Who could help laughing? Whether her listeners were of Chinese ancestry or Italian, whether they lived in the slums or the luxury apartments that were all part of the diverse 19th District, a ripple of amusement would spread through the crowd as Bella beamed on them cheerfully. The political reporters covering her campaign grinned, too. For with this kind of candidate, their job was a breeze.

"She'd be terrific in show business," they told one another. And real stars like Barbra Striesand, who volunteered to raise money for Bella, obviously agreed. On this one point, so did her political enemies. "She'd do great as a nightclub comic," one of them wrote scornfully. Even Bella's mother, still going strong at the age of eighty-three, would tell her neighbors she used to think this daughter would become an actress.

Among Bella's friends, though, there were some who took the problems of the world so seriously that they were distressed by her dramatic style. Wasn't it a bad idea to treat politics as a branch of show business? Besides her jokes, another thing she did gave them the same uneasy feeling. In front of any audience, even when she was just striding through a supermarket shaking hands with shoppers, she seemed different from her usual self—her arm-waving gestures were exaggerated, her voice was not merely louder but it also had much more of a typical New York accent to it. You couldn't really say she was acting, and yet she surely gave the impression of being somehow larger than life.

That's right! Other friends of Bella's were perfectly willing to concede all this. According to them, there was a close link between show business and politics, as practically every President had demonstrated. When John F. Kennedy had worked a sort of magic on a majority of the American public, convincing canny White House correspondents along with carefree teen-agers that he was a twentieth-century knight in shining armor, his brand of magic had been called charisma. But no matter what you called it, a person who wanted to accomplish something important politically had to have a talent for reaching voters' emotions.

And Bella had a particularly difficult challenge, these friends would say. As a woman, she first had to dispel the lingering prejudice against women in politics still held by a lot of female as well as male voters. Furthermore, she'd been a feminist long before the new women's liberation movement had frightened so many conservatives—so even if she could happily count on the support of her liberated sisters, she was bound to face a highly negative reaction from the people of either sex who ridiculed the whole struggle for equal rights more and more bitterly now that the movement was gaining increasing strength.

On top of everything else, Bella Abzug also had to cope with a basic fact of American politics. Even in New York City, where radical ideas had always taken root more readily than in most other parts of the country, the average person was deeply suspicious of anybody who wanted to shake up the established system. Speaking out for a specific change, such as improving the treatment of racial minorities, could gain votes among the numerous liberals and from the minority groups affected. But ever since her exciting years at Hunter, Bella had boldly led one radical cause after another. So she must be a Communist, a lot of people assumed.

"Bella, were you ever a Communist?" reporters frequently asked her.

"*No!*" But no matter how often she denied the charge, some people still said she was lying, while others said that even if she hadn't actually joined the Communist party she'd been so closely connected with subversive groups at various stages in her career that she couldn't be trusted. It wasn't just Archie Bunker types who talked about her this way, either. People who prided themselves on being fair-minded seemed surprisingly ready to believe the worst about this woman.

For she was rude and pushy, many of them had read in their newspapers. She used gutter language, it was claimed. Noisy. Aggressive. Ugly. All of these, plus some even less appealing words, had frequently been muttered about her by her political enemies.

But instead of trying to tell people she wasn't as horrible as they'd heard, Bella showed them the minute she met them what kind of a person she really was. If they could just see that she was a human being, maybe a little different from themselves in some ways, and yet no fire-breathing dragon to be afraid of, then she could hope to get across her real message.

So she'd start every speech with a little clowning, then as soon as she sensed a friendly feeling coming from her audience—"good vibes," her kids would say—she'd lean forward and launch into a rousing political appeal. Sometimes she'd have her speech already written, but she never read it word for word or did more than just glance at it every so often to make sure she wasn't leaving out an important point. Her experience in courtrooms had taught her that she did much better if she let herself talk naturally, and she might decide on the spur of the moment about the best way to express what she wanted to communicate.

"You know," she might confide, "I really am a very serious woman. I am not being funny now"—and her voice would become deeply earnest—"I am not being a bit funny when I say that the real enemies in this country are the Pentagon and its pals in big business."

Jabbing a finger into the air, she'd go on:

"It's no joke to me that women in this country are terribly oppressed and are made to suffer economic, legal, and social discrimination.

"I am not giving you a wild fantasy when I claim that I'm going to help organize a new political coalition of the women, the minorities and the young people, along with the poor, the elderly, the workers and the unemployed, which is going to turn this country upside down and inside out.

"We're going to reclaim our cities, create more

jobs, better housing, better health care, more child-care centers, more help for drug addicts.

"We're going to start doing something for the millions of people in this country whose needs, because of the callousness of the men who've been running our government, have taken a low priority to the cost of killing people in Indochina."

Then she'd pause as if to let her listeners know she understood that they had to think over what she'd said. Her voice softer, she would continue:

"You think all this sounds somewhat grandiose? But let me tell you something." Now her voice would be rising again.

"This is the only thing we *can* do and still survive. It's not *my* master plan. It's what half a million people in this district—Puerto Ricans, Jews, Italians, Chinese, Irish, Poles, Russians, blacks, even old-fashioned white Anglo-Saxon Americans—it's what you've been telling me as I walk the streets.

"You have had it! That's what I keep hearing. You're fed up, you've almost lost hope. The mood of the country is one place and its government is someplace else. One poll after another shows that vast numbers of people in this country are against this rotten war.

"Well, I'm going to work to stop it. I don't intend to disappear in Congress. I'm an activist. I want to bring Congress back to the people...."

By now, Bella Abzug's voice would have stirred a great wave of applause that drowned out whatever else she intended to say. With a satisfied smile, she'd wait for it to subside before cheerfully telling everybody which lever on the voting machine to pull on Election Day. Shaking dozens of outstretched hands as she started toward the exit, she would feel incredibly refreshed, even though she'd been going without a stop almost since the sun rose and now it was nearly midnight.

When she didn't have a meeting scheduled, she'd be out on the street with her endless handshaking. She drove herself at such a pace that even the patient Martin protested she'd ruin her health. But she couldn't rest, she was too keyed up, and she couldn't help pushing her staff to work just as hard as she did.

So she had hundreds of volunteers out every day, covering every neighborhood in the district. Her headquarters in Greenwich Village doubled as a day-care center where mothers left their kids while they rang doorbells for Bella. Older kids, including her own, gave out leaflets and buttons. Sound trucks blasted her message above the traffic noises on the main shopping avenues.

All this effort paid off. After the polls closed on November 3, it didn't take long for the results to be tabulated. By nearly ten thousand votes, Bella Abzug had beaten her Republican opponent.

The minute her victory was official, glaring lights flashed on and a television interviewer spoke into his microphone. "Ladies and gentlemen," he said, "here

Bella Abzug and her family during her first campaign for Congress. *Courtesy of Congresswoman Abzug*

is Mrs. Bella Abzug, the new Democratic Congressman—"

"Congress*woman*," Bella interrupted in her deepest voice, and everybody in the crowd broke up.

Throughout the campaign, Martin had stayed in the background but he was with his wife that night and he was asked to say a few words to her supporters. "I hope you deserve her," he remarked simply.

The candidate's mother was also present. "I always knew Bella would make it," Mrs. Savitzky said. "She always did her homework and practiced her violin without being told to."

But it was the usually shy Egee who brought the biggest response from the crowd. Bella's older daughter didn't have to remind anybody there that her mother's slogan had been, "This woman's place is in the House—the House of Representatives." All that Egee said when she stood up with a big smile was, "Thank God we're getting her out of *our* house and into *their* House."

9

Rocking the Boat

On January 21, 1971, the new Ninety-second Congress convened for the first time. In the imposing chamber of the House of Representatives, there was the usual ceremony administering the oath of office to the 435 members elected from every part of the country. Among them, New York's Bella Abzug had already stirred the greatest curiosity.

Even such a minor matter as what she'd be wearing excited lively gossip. Would she dare to appear on the floor of the House in one of her famous hats? No, she did not.

"But didn't you hear?" A reporter who particularly enjoyed starting juicy rumors told the whole press gallery that Bella had actually tried to break the rule forbidding hats. And when "Fishbait"

Miller, the official doorkeeper, had asked her to remove her headgear, she'd replied with a remark that couldn't be printed.

It wasn't true, of course. As soon as she'd arrived in Washington, Bella had studied the rules of the House very carefully. A long time ago, when she'd been on the Hunter student council, she'd learned how much you could accomplish if you knew all about the procedure governing a lawmaking body. Now she had a lot of urgent business she wanted this Congress to act on, and if she could figure out a way to force Nixon to stop killing innocent people over in Asia, she'd willingly park her hat in the cloakroom.

Nevertheless, that ridiculous story of her alleged dirty language became an instant legend on Capitol Hill. It almost seemed as though most of her new colleagues wished she could be laughed away as a foul-mouthed freak, definitely not a lady and not likely, either, to become "one of the boys" in this exclusive club.

Well, Bella had always refused to play the part of an old-fashioned lady, and she certainly could use some choice cuss words when she lost her temper. Furthermore, she had no desire to win a place in the inner circles of Congress. Her aim was to shake it up, not to fit in quietly. But anybody who thought she'd bother with such childishness as insulting poor old Fishbait was going to be surprised. No, she had a lot of other and much better ideas.

So right after the formal swearing-in, she hurried

Rocking the Boat

out to the Capitol steps. Six hundred cheering delegates from the Women Strike for Peace were waiting for her there, along with a few hundred other people from other peace groups. Shirley Chisholm, the black Congresswoman who represented another New York City district, was holding a sheet of paper.

Then Bella Abzug raised her right hand again, while her friend Shirley Chisholm read the words of a special peace oath. In this second swearing-in, Bella pledged "to work for new priorities to heal the domestic wounds of war and to use our country's wealth for life, not death."

As she finished her pledge, some teen-agers from Harlem held up a banner: "GIVE 'EM HELLA, BELLA!" A cluster of elderly Congressmen who had come out to see what was going on looked quite shaken already. Nothing like this had ever happened before, as far as any of them could remember.

Yet that was only the beginning. By the end of her first day in office, Bella had broken the unwritten law limiting first-term legislators to just listening during their entire term, and she'd introduced a resolution which made reporters grab their pencils. It was the official policy of the House Democratic leadership to go along with President Nixon's program for "winding down" the Vietnam war at his own pace. But Congresswoman Abzug had the nerve to defy her own party's leaders, as well as the President, and to call for a total withdrawal of all American troops from Indochina no later than July 4.

She also announced that, despite various efforts to discourage her, she intended to fight for a seat on the House's powerful Armed Services Committee. This choice assignment rarely went to a woman because the leadership thought health or education was a more suitable subject for female lawmakers to debate. And even a male liberal would have to convince his party's leaders that he could be trusted not to rock the boat if he were to be taken aboard. Yet here was a woman who'd been bragging all over Washington about rocking the boat, boldly demanding a change in the usual system for selecting committee members.

"It's not going to be easy," Bella admitted in her diary on her first evening in Washington.

But it certainly did make the national scene more interesting to have Bella Abzug there. Her brash request for such an important committee assignment gave television a good reason to feature her on all sorts of programs from the nightly news to talk shows, and she took full advantage of her opportunities.

"First of all," she briskly explained to one of her hosts, "the tradition down here is that new members, like myself, take what they get. In other words, we are expected to defer to the seniority system, which dictates that we shut up and listen to the tired old men who run this government."

As a result, the Armed Services Committee was loaded with reactionaries, she went on. They only listened to pro-military witnesses, and their main interest was in getting juicy defense contracts for factories in their own districts.

"Well, this is appalling!" Bella exploded. "The House committee should challenge the military—not speak for it. Those admirals and generals and munitions-makers should have to answer for themselves, every step of the way—"

But then she was interrupted for a commercial, and the program's producer came out to tell her she was being too rough on some respected figures. Would she please let up, he asked.

"What do you want me to talk about?" she shot back. "Tulips?"

Bella's plain speaking delighted some people as much as it offended others, though, and she was heartened by getting quite a bit of favorable publicity. For instance, columnist Mary McGrory wrote a piece headed "BELLA Vs. THE HOUSE" that gave the readers of major newspapers around the country a new perspective: "She's zestful and funny, and although a Women's Libber, wears outrageous hats and French perfume . . . 'She's nice to talk to,' said a wondering and conventional House member. 'I was really surprised after what I had heard.' "

It may not have struck many of the readers of that article that there might be a simple way of explaining why they were receiving a different impression of Bella Abzug from the usual "Battling Bella" ridicule. But nobody who stopped to think a minute could be mystified. For the world of politics was almost completely a man's world—on every level. In political reporting, just as in the whole process of running the country, women had a hard time getting beyond the lowest rung of the ladder.

So Mary McGrory was one of the few women who had managed to win widespread respect as a political analyst. She's just defending Bella because one female has to stick up for another, some people assumed. Let's put it another way, Bella's staff suggested. When even a fair-minded man sits down to write about a woman who dares to speak out, he may feel threatened. After all, if other women learn to talk back to their lords and masters, what'll happen to men's special privileges? Consciously or unconsciously, a lot of male reporters make her seem repulsive. But a woman writer isn't threatened by Bella; a woman can really be fair-minded. Okay, it's possible that a woman writer will root for Bella from a sense of sisterhood. Well, what's wrong with that? Men do the same thing constantly. Still, it can't be merely sisterly loyalty that'll persuade an experienced person like Mary McGrory to call a new member of Congress an overnight celebrity.

The big question in Washington, McGrory wrote soon after the new Congress convened, was: "How long will it take to box Bella in?"

For the House leaders had plenty of tactics for squashing any rebel, as Bella herself was well aware.

So she'd come on pretty strong the very first day to prove it wouldn't be easy to stop her. "Bella knows she's moving in a minefield," McGrory remarked, then let Bella explain:

> "I know they'll smile at me, that's their style, and kick me in the teeth the minute I get out of line . . .
>
> "I'm here a week," she says with a grin, "and nothing has changed. But I'll be in there pitching every step of the way."

And she certainly was. After ten years of protesting on the sidewalk outside of the White House, she got a routine invitation to attend a reception there for freshmen members of Congress. Should she go? Sure, it might give her a chance to score a few points. So she called Martin and asked him if he'd like to fly down to go with her, instead of waiting to hear all about it when she flew home for the weekend. By all means, he said; even though he didn't much enjoy following her around Washington, he might as well see the place where he'd be First Man one of these days.

On the afternoon before the party, Bella took an hour off to have her hair done in the House beauty parlor. Of the eleven women who'd been elected to Congress the preceding November, Louise Day Hicks of Boston was about the furthest from Bella politically, but this ardent conservative sat under the next dryer and proved that sisterhood could rise above politics. "What are you going to wear tomorrow?" she asked Bella. "Long or short?"

At the moment, Bella hadn't made up her mind, but when she tape-recorded her diary entry for the big night she confessed: "I decided to wear a short dress so I could also wear a hat. I didn't want to deprive the President of that great event. I figured I'd let him see me in my whole regalia."

Then, after describing the problem she and Martin had in finding the right gate to the White House, she went on:

> When we finally got there, it was all red carpet and long gown and dapper people. With all the regalia, it actually looked more British than American to us. We got a big kick out of it. With the Marine band playing in the background, we started up the gold and marble steps and lo and behold . . .
>
> There He Was. His Wife Too. Even though there wasn't a camera in sight, he had his makeup on. We got in the reception line and then . . .
>
> "Oh," he said. "I've been looking forward to meeting you."
>
> "President Nixon," I said, unsmiling, "I want you to know that my constituents want you to withdraw from Vietnam and they're unhappy that you haven't."

Rocking the Boat

Whereupon his hand stiffened up immensely and locked mine into what Martin described as an Indian hand wrestle.

"We're doing better than our predecessors," he said.

"Well, your predecessors didn't do very well, but you're doing worse."

He stiffened up further, and his whole body became sort of rigid. "Yes, yes," he said, and pushed me on to Pat.

"Oh, I've been looking forward to meeting you," she chirped. "I've read all about you and your cute little bonnets."

So at least Bella had the satisfaction of telling Richard Nixon right to his face what she thought about his war policies. She had the satisfaction, too, during her first winter in Washington of welding more than thirty other Representatives into a solid pressure group for peace. They not only joined her in co-sponsoring her resolution calling for a pull-out of all American troops, they also could be counted on to support her in the dizzy maneuvers the leadership kept thinking up to try to squelch her.

Still, she certainly couldn't claim to be making a whole lot of headway. Just as she'd expected, the top brass in her own party refused to go to bat for her, and she didn't get onto the Armed Services Committee. While she accomplished something by calling attention to the unfair system of favoritism the insiders got away with in running Congress, she had to take Government Operations and Public Works as her two committee assignments. Actually, these were pretty good for a first-termer, everyone told her, so maybe she would be able to stir up a little action after all.

Yet, on the main issue of ending the war she was constantly batting her head against a stone wall. Of course, the powers behind the scenes were bent on keeping her peace resolution from even coming up for a vote. When she saw what a job she'd have smoking out these hawks, she changed the date by which the withdrawal had to be finished to December 31. In March, she got the unofficial caucus of House Democrats to consider her measure, and in their balloting she was just two shy of a majority. That really scared the leadership. With the Democratic caucus on record in favor of her resolution, it would be awfully hard to prevent a vote on the House floor. Then her enemies counterattacked.

Month after month, they played one trick after another to stop the caucus from supporting her. For several months in a row, the business of the caucus was practically suspended so that there couldn't be another vote on the Abzug resolution.

Then Bella changed her own tactics. Since her goal was to get the House itself to act, she'd simply bypass the caucus. It wasn't for nothing that she'd studied the rules so carefully, and now she went back to the book to check up on a terrific idea. Yup, there were about forty-seven different kinds of questions any member could force the House to consider—*without having them funneled first through some committee that would surely block them.*

But only "a resolution of inquiry" got this special privilege. Anything called just a "resolution" could be stymied forever by a committee. Okay, instead of a resolution about withdrawing from Vietnam, she'd propose a resolution of inquiry on the situation there. At least that would bring the subject into the open, and with the peace movement gaining new strength every week, some of these timid doves in Congress might get the courage to support her.

Then from the inquiry, the House could proceed to cut off all funds for the war and to order all troops home by a certain date. And Nixon *would have to obey*.

So Bella prepared her inquiry, put it in the proper slot, and alerted her staff to keep an extra-close watch on the House's activities. While she prided herself about being present more often than practically any other member, the schedule of committee hearings made for frequent conflicts. If you took your committee work seriously, you just had to miss some routine sessions of the House itself. But when that inquiry came up, Bella Abzug was positively going to be on hand to defend it.

At last she heard that it would reach the floor the following day, although nobody could be certain exactly when. Since the House convened at noon,

Bella left her office about ten minutes to twelve but she didn't think she had to hurry. What with the opening prayer and the normal procedure of allowing one-minute speeches by members who had something to say on any subject, no real business was ever transacted until about half-past twelve.

As Bella strode along a corridor toward the basement tunnel connecting her office building with the Capitol, she passed a ladies' room. Figuring that she had plenty of time, she stopped there for a minute or two—and arrived on the floor of the House at three minutes after noon.

It was too late.

Just on this particular day, the presiding officer had not let anybody make a one-minute speech. He'd called up Bella's inquiry the instant the prayer ended. Another member rose immediately and moved that the inquiry be tabled by a voice vote. The handful of members present murmured "Aye." In no time flat, the plan Bella had had such hopes for was dead and buried.

As soon as she discovered what had happened, Bella did lose her temper. She stormed around the chamber, trying desperately to arrange some way of reversing her defeat. Obviously, though, this dirty trick had been planned in advance, and the leadership wasn't about to allow any second thoughts. Out in the cloakroom that afternoon, Congresswoman Abzug amply proved that the stories concerning her vocabulary of swear words weren't all invented. "I've never felt so badly about anything in my whole life," she told her diary later.

But even if she failed in her main effort, Bella bounced back as she always had. Now that she was in Congress, she could do more than ever before on behalf of the causes she believed in—and a lot of people, including her own staff, thought that nobody there worked harder than she did.

Because peace was her foremost goal, she gave it top priority. Despite being frozen out of the Armed Services Committee, she formed an unofficial committee to hold hearings at which anti-war witnesses got their first chance to speak up on Capitol Hill. She took advantage of the House rules giving Representatives the right to be heard by any official committee, and testified herself when any war-related measure was being considered. She also organized a group of Congressional doves who flew all over the country, appearing at dozens of peace rallies.

When thousands of young peace activists descended on Washington, the President of the United States got so alarmed that he took steps that violated the Constitution he'd sworn to uphold. Police were ordered to make mass arrests, grabbing everybody in sight and herding them into a fenced-in football field without food, water, or any sanitary facilities. No legal charges were filed against any of these people. The police didn't even bother to list their names.

And Bella Abzug, almost alone in the whole city

of Washington, roared out a protest. Sure, the leaders of the demonstration had threatened to tie up traffic. They'd said they wanted to stop the government for a day because the government had refused to listen to the people who were demanding peace. This kind of activity could bring on violence, Bella admitted, and violence was not her thing.

But whatever some of the kids might have done, the police did much worse. Like the Gestapo in Nazi Germany, they didn't obey any law themselves. They just seized people right and left, whether they were demonstrators or innocent bystanders. Every person arrested needed a lawyer badly, so Bella got busy.

First she had one of her aides call a friend who did traffic reports for a local radio station. Could he fly her to the football field in his helicopter? He could, and when they landed, police and soldiers with bayonets surrounded them.

"Step aside!" Bella hollered. "I'm Congresswoman Abzug, and I'm going to see what's going on here."

She did, and for the next several days she pulled every string she could to get fair treatment for the thousands who'd been arrested. She told their story to reporters, she went to court herself, she defended them at a tense rally on the Capitol steps. Many Nixon supporters attacked her because they said the President was right to act decisively against the threat of violence. But even one of Nixon's firmest backers, when pressed by reporters, admitted that conditions in the emergency outdoor prison on the

Congresswoman Abzug at a Martin Luther King Day church service. *Jean Wolcott photo*

football field should have bothered the President's opponents. "Nobody in the Democratic party was down there except Bella Abzug," Republican Senator Hugh Scott said. "She's the only man in the House."

That made Bella grin. "Isn't that interesting?" she

asked her diary. "In his male terms, it must mean that I'm the only one who has any guts around here."

Yet nobody could imagine that Bella ever forgot she was a female. In her election campaign, she'd kept saying that women made up more than half of the population, and they deserved a lot more attention from the nation's lawmakers. During her first term, she spread the same message tirelessly.

She testified at committee hearings in favor of the proposed Equal Rights Amendment to the Constitution. With Shirley Chisholm, she sponsored a bill for broad federal support of day-care centers where working mothers could leave their children safely. In her large handbag stuffed with papers, she always carried the draft of a clause forbidding any discrimination against women—so she was always ready to move that such a clause be added when any measure involving government spending was being debated.

Most important of all, though, she worked closely with the leaders of every branch of the women's movement on an idea that had been in the back of her mind for a long time. If women were ever going to get any real political power, she thought, they would have to learn how to work together more effectively. Finally, in July of 1971, she had the great pleasure of sitting on the platform when the National Women's Political Caucus held its first meeting.

Bella's picture was on the front page of *The New*

York Times then, along with a headline three columns wide:

WOMEN ORGANIZE FOR POLITICAL POWER
by Eileen Shanahan

Washington, July 10—More than 200 women—Republicans, Democrats and independents—met today to inaugurate a new organization aimed at increasing the number of women holding public office. . . .

But around the same time, some men who were very powerful politically in the state of New York were hatching a different plan. Their aim was to *decrease* the number of women in Congress, by making sure that Representative Bella Abzug had almost no chance to win re-election the following year.

10
Exit?

It was no secret that the inner core of New York City was losing population. For several years, everyone with a special interest in politics had had to accept a sad fact. After the 1970 census report was released, the political map of Manhattan would have to be changed—and instead of four districts, each sending its own representative to Congress, there would be only three.

Ordinarily, this prospect could be expected to cause much anguish among political leaders. But during 1971, satisfied smiles appeared on the faces of many important figures in both major parties. Rumors about why those men were smiling spread widely, and the rumors turned out to be true. At the beginning of 1972, a column in the *Washington Post* by Nicholas Von Hoffman started:

> Bella of the wide-brimmed hat has been up in New York snorting, ripping and letting it be known she will not die dainty. "I don't plan to let that gang of enemies cut me down," she was saying from the ruins of her congressional district. For Bella Abzug hasn't been redistricted, she has been de-districted, her old constituency cut up and split in four different ways.
>
> She has been demolished, the political map redesigned to put her out of politics forever. She says she's going to fight back and fight on, and maybe she will and maybe she will win. She is Bella, after all, but that's why Nelson Rockefeller and the conservative Democrats wanted to get her and beat her brains out. They did indeed liquidate her inelegantly because, as she says, "When you have all the power, you don't need to be clever."
>
> Why they did it is interesting. Bella has zilch seniority, nor is she regarded as being especially effective in Congress. She has stood for something, however. There is in her chemistry an uncrackable element which resists being reduced to the House of Repre-

sentatives' ordinary bipartisan sludge. That makes her dangerous. She attracts people excites them, gets them into politics, and if there were too many like her, we would begin to discern a difference in our two major political parties. . . .

Bella did enjoy reading that column, for here was someone who really understood what she was all about. By now there were more than a few others, too, with the sense to grasp the fact that she stood for something important. Wonder of wonders, *Life* Magazine put her picture on their cover in June, and they even used a decent close-up, showing that even if she was no movie star, her face still wouldn't frighten little children the way her enemies claimed.

And did she ever have enemies in this spring of 1972!

Any sane person would stay out of politics, she sometimes thought. In the first place, it was bad for your health when you skipped meals and grabbed a few hot dogs or candy bars while you rushed around sixteen hours a day as she always seemed to be doing. Already she'd been laid up twice, most recently with pneumonia only a few months after being hurried to the hospital suffering from just plain exhaustion. But, being Bella, she couldn't merely rest in the Bethesda medical center where members of Congress were treated. Nope, the young navy guys who took care of nursing duties there were so curious

Bella Abzug and New York's Lieutenant Governor Mary Anne Krupsak campaigning for voters on a Long Island beach. *Courtesy of Congresswoman Abzug's office*

about her, they kept asking her about women's lib, or the war, or why she'd run for office. So she'd talk on and on—loving every minute, she'd have to admit. Wherever she went, the same kind of thing happened. People had been fed so many myths about her that when they saw her they bombarded her with questions, which she couldn't help getting involved in answering because she wanted them to realize she was a human being like themselves, not some type of freak as they'd been told.

Still, all this attention pretty much cut her off from any normal activities. She couldn't even go shopping for a new dress without being surrounded, and if she went to a restaurant, strangers kept coming up "Bella, Bella, Bella"-ing her every minute. The worst thing, though, was the strain on her family life.

No matter that it was Mother's Day, the telephone kept ringing so that her sister Helene, living the suburban life out on Long Island and still teaching music, had to do double duty looking after Ma. As for Bella's own daughters, Egee at Hofstra and Liz at Boston University, they didn't need her now the way they had when they were younger, but having a famous mother was rough on them, no doubt about it. Naturally, they didn't like attracting special attention because of their mother, and they would much rather have lived their own lives instead of being forced to trail along in her shadow.

So Bella made a point of not asking them to make political appearances with her. Heaven forbid, she didn't want any Nixon-style Julie or Tricia dolls in her family. Once when she was talking to a group of Girl Scouts, a youngster asked her why her daughters hadn't come too, and Bella grinned. "Does your mother drag you with her every place she goes?" she demanded.

Nevertheless, it was impossible to pretend that Egee and Liz weren't suffering some special pangs. If they all got together to celebrate either girl's birthday, a political emergency was bound to erupt. Sure, they both got a kick out of the whirlwind atmosphere that always seemed to accompany their mother, but neither of them could ever have the comfort of her undivided attention. They didn't suffer nearly as much, though, as their father did.

When Bella thought of what she owed to Martin, tears often filled her eyes. Yet this was usually something like crying from happiness because she couldn't get over how lucky she'd been to find such a husband. Without his love and encouragement, she couldn't possibly have carried on, and she wanted everybody to know how remarkable he was.

"Martin's a very independent person," she would tell interviewers. "He's strong and he's smart. It's difficult to talk of"—and her voice would sound softer, more emotional—"but I wish I could because he's an unsung hero."

However, since she'd been in Congress, more than once her tears had been real. People could be so cruel! Why did they think it was funny to introduce him as *Mrs.* Martin Abzug? Just because some men couldn't stand to see their wives in the limelight, it didn't mean all men were that insecure. Martin didn't like being apart from Monday to Thursday every week any more than she did, but besides his stockbroking job he had lots of friends, he went to plays and movies, he loved to watch any sport on TV, he definitely was not a meek little man—but when he did go with her on some weekend political thing, the way a few idiots talked to him was disgraceful. While he was perfectly capable of holding his own, she hated having him ridiculed. Of course, the most vicious abuse was aimed right in her direction, though, and it could be awful.

For instance, the show put on by those big-shot reporters whose club was called the Inner Circle. Knowing that no women had been allowed to attend one of these yearly performances until recently, Bella had been tempted to pass up any event with such a sexist history. "Would that I had!" she later told friends.

In the first act, she said, an oaf from the *Daily News* came out on the stage with his shoulders and rear end padded very substantially. He was wearing a satin blouse and a skirt with a gaudy flower pattern. On his head was a large floppy hat. He was obviously supposed to be Bella. Accompanying him was a fellow playing the part of Mayor Lindsay, who said:

"I stole two elections, but how the hell did you win?"

The character representing Bella flounced around a minute before replying with a leer, "I have broad-based support," and then broke out into song:

Exit? 119

> I guess I've never been the high-fashioned kind,
> Mother Nature gave me a big behind.
> Oh, I'm filled with jubilation
> For women's liberation
> We rang our liberty bell
> We'll burn a bra and girdle
> But dammit there's one hurdle
> When we take them off
> We all look like hell. . . .

And then out came somebody in a frilly white apron with a sign around his neck saying—wouldn't you know?—*Mrs. Martin Abzug.*

Bella was so furious that she felt like jumping up and leaving as a protest. Political criticism she could take—any person in politics had to, especially if you dished it out the way she did. But this was something else. It wasn't just a mean attack against her, it was attack against all women, because it singled out her physical appearance as the only subject worth considering. Whenever men did that, they were really saying that the only important fact about any woman was whether or not she looked sexy. So this was pure male chauvinist piggery. And why should she let those guys get away with it?

But she didn't walk out. Before she'd made up her mind, half a dozen people from other tables were swooping down on her, urging her not to get upset by such garbage. There were still tears in her eyes, but suddenly Bella was grinning. "Who's upset?" she demanded, and she pounded a fist against her other hand to prove what a calm person she was.

She did a lot more pounding when she discovered how those great statesmen in Albany had torn apart her district. Of course, she'd known all along that they weren't going to make it easy for her to run again—the whole world knew it. But the bare-faced knifing, like a murder committed in broad daylight, really hurt her. Nobody even bothered to pretend that the three men and the one woman most affected by the redistricting were being treated equally. "Get Bella!" That was their war cry, and they might as well have shouted it from the rooftops. What kind of country was this anyway? Why should she knock herself out trying to do some good? If she'd just quit, she and Martin could take a long vacation....

Quit? Bella Abzug quit? Oh, no, she would not, and down would come that fist. For her only real question was: Which of the new districts should she run in?

From one standpoint, it didn't matter. Each of the three men involved had promised to seek another term, so she'd have to fight in a primary first unless she took a big chance and ran as an independent. But if the primary route was rough, it was still safer than trying to get elected without being the official candidate of the Democratic party. All right, she'd enter a primary.

Among her three possible opponents, two were liberals. Some of her friends thought she ought to go after the conservative candidate because he deserved defeat. However, the district he represented was mainly on Staten Island, with a comparatively small chunk of her territory now added to it. They were nice people over on the island, but they'd much rather vote for you if your name was Murphy, which happened to be the name of their present Congressman. So Bella shook her head. If she had to fight, she was certainly going to fight to win.

That meant she'd better pick the new 20th District, which had the largest number of her own people besides being where she lived. But she'd have quite a problem here, too. His name was William Fitts Ryan.

Bill Ryan not only had one of the best voting records in the House of Representatives, by Bella's standards; he was also a very nice man, if a little on the quiet side for her taste. And there was a particular reason why she hated to challenge him. About a year before, he'd had a serious cancer operation, supposedly curing him, but everybody in politics knew that wasn't true.

Every political reporter in town had the story, too, and yet it didn't get printed. All of those allegedly hard-boiled characters were holding back because Bill Ryan himself didn't realize how sick he was, and nobody wanted to be the one to tell him. Well, Bella wouldn't tell him, either.

Still, she felt she had no choice except to announce that she was running against Ryan in the primary on June 20. She did this early in April. Bella had expected a large amount of negative reaction after she released her statement, and she thought she'd be able to handle it without any great difficulty. The uproar would simmer down in a couple of days, she assured her friends.

But it didn't.

That Bill Ryan stopped talking to her wasn't any surprise, but even the steadfast *Village Voice* deserted her. "Is it worth it, Bella?" the paper from her own neighborhood demanded: "Is it really worth it?"

She tried to answer calmly that despite Ryan's liberal beliefs, he didn't provide the kind of leadership she did. "I'm an activist and Bill isn't," she said. "It's as simple as that." But practically everybody seemed to think she'd started a civil war, and whether she liked it or not, that's what the campaign turned into.

Then, of course, the Nixon fans had a field day. On the front page of the *Wall Street Journal*, they could read:

"I'm More Liberal
Than You'll Ever Be!"
"Oh Yeah? Says Who?"

****

Two Super-Liberals Go At It
In New York Congress Race
By Norman C. Miller

New York—It has to be one of the strangest campaign slogans ever. The voters, proclaims the candidate, have a chance to choose "the greater of two goods."

And the self-styled greater of the two goods, otherwise known as Congresswoman Bella Abzug, doesn't mind sailing into another super-liberal to give the voters that choice—and to try to save her House seat in the bargain.

For Mrs. Abzug—who has rocketed to fame as a bellicose dove and women's-lib advocate though she's only in her first term—is running in the June 20 primary against one of the few other Congressmen as far out as she is, veteran Rep. William Fitts Ryan.

Thanks to a Republican gerrymander that obliterated Mrs. Abzug's old district, Mr. Ryan and the leather-lunged lady are engaged in a bizarre and bitter contest here on Manhattan's West Side. And in this seedbed of extreme anti-war activism, they're vying to outdo each other with schemes that would be dismissed as kooky almost anywhere else.

The other day, for instance, Mrs. Abzug came up with a bright idea: why not end the war by impeaching President Nixon? So she announced her plan to the House. Moments later, though, a smug Rep. Ryan was on his feet with a proud announcement that he already had filed an impeachment resolution.

While this sort of thing has made both pariahs in the stodgy House, it goes over big here on the West Side. At the moment, though, what's even bigger is the feud among the liberal activists choosing sides in the Abzug-Ryan duel. They're bombarding one another with invective they usually reserve for Mr. Nixon and his kind.*

Actually, it was the supporters of both candidates who got sufficiently carried away to fling around words like "traitor." Ryan, a shy man with no gift for street campaigning even when he felt well, stayed mostly in Washington. And Bella, out on the streets every spare minute, made a real effort to explain why she was running.

It was terribly unfair to set up one set of standards for male candidates and another for females, she kept insisting. If any *man* had decided to oppose Ryan, she said, most voters wouldn't have been the least bit surprised or upset. Ryan's close friends might have felt angry, but even they would probably have shrugged and told each other, "That's politics." Yet a woman, apparently, was not supposed to run against anyone doing a reasonably good job—no matter that she really believed she could do better. Well, Bella maintained, this kind of double standard didn't make sense.

* Reprinted by permission of the *Wall Street Journal* © 1972 Dow Jones & Co., Inc. All rights reserved.

"Why should there just be eleven women in Congress?" she'd demand. "Why should I be told either to retire or go into a race I can't win? The voters have the right to make that decision, not Rockefeller or any other boss."

But nobody seemed to be paying much attention. They were making too much noise themselves, about morality and ego trips and what a sweet guy Bill Ryan was. It got louder and louder throughout April and May and early June. All over Manhattan, people Bella had been counting on joined the enemy camp.

"Mrs. Abzug is fighting the wrong man at the wrong time in the wrong district," Roslyn Willett said. And who was she? The chairperson of a very small branch of—the *Women's* Political Caucus. Although Gloria Steinem and a good many others stood firm, Bella felt as if the ground were sinking below her feet.

So she hollered louder herself. "That's a lot of baloney!" she shouted when a truck driver told her she was no better than Ryan, she just talked more. "That's a complete and utter lie," she insisted when Ryan aides blamed her for a whispering campaign about their candidate's health. "My people have been under instructions not to discuss Ryan's health under any circumstances," Bella said. "The charge is being raised by the Ryan people just as a way to try to get a sympathy vote for him."

Whatever the reason, the thin and pale Ryan did arouse plenty of sympathy. On June 20, 1972, he beat Bella Abzug in the Democratic primary, by a margin of more than two to one.

It was a terrible disappointment, but Bella took her defeat gracefully. She went over to Ryan headquarters as soon as the verdict was official, and she not only congratulated him, she promised to support him in November.

Then back at her own headquarters, she gamely rallied her glum supporters. "Don't go far away," she told them. "We'll all be back together again soon."

Did that mean she had some plans to run for another office? Reporters crowded around her, seeking a hint of what she'd do next. In another year, the city would be electing a new mayor, and would she get into that contest? "I'm not making any announcements now," Bella said, smiling. "I don't want to scare everyone all over again." So if they had to write something, they could just say she and Martin would be taking a nice long vacation.

But now that she'd lost, the campaign bitterness seemed to evaporate. In *Newsweek* Magazine there was a story headed "EXIT BELLA," which described how she'd been "quickly turned out of Congress after only one term," and it sounded sorry to see her depart. Without her, politics wouldn't be as lively, although people should have been absorbed by the presidential election coming up in a few months. Yet, almost everyone appeared to assume that Richard Nixon would win a second term, especially after the Democrats chose Senator George McGovern as their candidate.

Naturally, Bella hoped that McGovern would somehow make it. Despite all sorts of bumbling and stumbling, he'd be a million times better than Nixon, and she agreed to direct a Women for McGovern committee with Shirley MacLaine, the actress. Then suddenly, less than three months after her own defeat, her whole future changed.

Bill Ryan really had been a very sick man, it turned out. For he died on September 17—and the Democratic party needed another candidate right away because it was only six weeks till Election Day. In such a case, there couldn't be a primary to let every registered voter make his or her choice. The decision was up to the heads of party committees from every neighborhood of Manhattan. By an overwhelming majority, they chose Bella Abzug.

But the bitter struggle earlier that year had not been forgotten. One person in particular could never forgive Bella. Priscilla Ryan, the widow of the man Bella had challenged, had always stayed in the background while her husband did his politicking, but now she came forth to do some challenging herself. With the support of a local party called the Liberals, which usually backed Democratic candidates, Mrs. Ryan announced that she was running for the seat her husband had held.

Privately, Bella muttered angrily. She thought Priscilla was letting herself be used as a sort of puppet by Bella's enemies, who would do anything to thwart her. And from the feminist viewpoint, it was disgusting when a bunch of men picked a woman candidate not because she was qualified but because they figured she would get a lot of sympathy and they could tell her how to vote after she got elected. *If* she got elected. Priscilla Ryan was a nice woman, but she was even shyer than her husband, she had to have a man with a bullhorn running around in front of her if she ever went out handshaking.

Still, Bella was very careful not to attack Priscilla publicly. She knew that some people were saying Bella Abzug was a heartless monster who'd driven Bill Ryan to an early grave by running against him. That was nonsense, of course—he'd died of cancer. But during the second Abzug-Ryan campaign, Bella Abzug seemed noticeably subdued.

"I hope Bella wins now," a professor who had been a strong supporter of Bill Ryan admitted. "She'll do a lot more in Congress than Priscilla ever could. But I hope she wins by just a few votes."

It didn't work out that way. There were three other candidates in the race—a Republican, a Conservative, and a member of the nearly invisible Socialist Workers party. Between them, they got a total of 28,000 votes. Priscilla Ryan got 43,000 votes. Bella Abzug got 85,500.

11
Back on the Hill

It's seven-thirty in the morning, and most of the people in the hotel coffee shop have newspapers propped up beside their plates. As the door from the lobby is flung open, eyes are raised around the room with a reflex glance of mild curiosity. These solitary figures who've been reading while they eat their breakfast are mainly men on business trips to Washington. Being strangers, they don't expect to recognize a familiar face, but they do.

Why, it's Bella! And isn't that good-looking gal with the glasses Gloria what's-her-name, the women's lib leader? It surely is, so during the next three quarters of an hour, everyone else on the scene keeps finding an excuse to stare in their direction. Except for stopping to sign a few autographs, though, Bella and her companion accomplish quite a lot, drafting a statement about a coming meeting of the Women's Political Caucus.

Then, by half past eight, Bella is climbing out of a cab in front of the huge building across from the Capitol where she has her office. Again heads turn to watch her progress, despite the fact that members of Congress are a common sight here. At the bank of elevators she stabs a button with the sign above it, "Members Only," then taps one foot impatiently. She's also swinging her big purse back and forth as if she's tempted to use it as a battering ram. A few men who look like bank officials join her. "You in a hurry, Bella?" one of them asks amiably. She glares at him because she's heard that this guy from Ohio has been making remarks about her shape.

"Hey, Bella!" a Louisiana Congressman says. "I prayed all night for you, honey."

She shrugs, but the corners of her mouth curve with amusement. "And why is that?" she asks.

"That you'd see the light!" He guffaws before adding: "It's like the gal who got in trouble, and met a priest. The priest said to her, 'I prayed all night for you last night.' And you know what she said? 'Why, fur fifteen cents I'd-a come over, honey.' "

Bella shakes her head while these brilliant colleagues of hers in the United States House of Representatives cackle gleefully. "What characters," she murmurs, yet she's smiling. How can you take such clowns seriously?

But when she finally reaches her office midway down a block-long corridor a few minutes later, she's not smiling. What a day this is going to be! Three separate committee hearings before lunch, plus the stack of urgent queries from her New York office she couldn't get to yesterday—and undoubtedly, five more sacks of mail have turned up overnight, even though most other members rarely receive more than one. She's also got about six dozen appointments already scheduled, without counting the tourists from her district bound to appear unannounced, merely wanting her to stop everything and hike out to the Capitol steps so they can snap pictures of her with their own camera. If somebody on her staff tells them she's too busy, they get insulted. Her wonderful staff, why they can't take more of the load off her shoulders she'll never understand.

"Where's Lee?" she's calling as she pulls her arms out of her coat sleeves in the little anteroom.

There are two other small rooms beyond the entry area, crowded with desks and filing cabinets. At the moment, several young people are typing or sorting papers while the receptionist talks softly into her telephone. It looks very peaceful, but the sound of Bella's voice seems to act like an electric current. Suddenly everyone is moving faster or talking louder, and a live wire of a woman appears in the doorway from the private inner office holding out a clipboard of message slips that almost crackle with urgency. This energetic person is Bella's administra-

One of the Congressional chores Bella Abzug enjoys is posing on the Capitol steps with groups of visiting students from her district. *Dev O'Neill photo*

tive assistant, or A.A., as the regulars on Capitol Hill refer to each member's chief of staff.

Lee is the third or fourth A.A. who's worked for Congresswoman Abzug in approximately three years, but nobody asks Bella about the exact number unless they want to see sparks fly. If there's any subject Bella feels the media have blown up unfairly, it's this topic of her staff problems. To say that people quit right and left simply isn't true, she sputters, listing the stalwarts who've been with her all along; for instance, Mim Kelber and Dora Friedman. Mim, a friend since high school, is her executive assistant up in New York, while Dora, who did such a great job for the reform wing of the Democratic party in New York, runs the main office where residents of the district can and do bring trillions of troubles.

All right, Washington has been more difficult but that's only natural when you're trying to accomplish so many different things, Bella will grumble. As on this particular day, with water pollution and mass transit and food stamps all being considered. "Oh, there you are, Lee," she says, throwing an arm around Lee's shoulder, then steering her into the inner private office. That door swings shut, and in the outer room a wary air of waiting settles on every face.

"I admire Bella more than anyone else in the House of Representatives," Jo Ellen, a college senior who's spending a semester as an intern here, tells a writer observing the daily routine. "It's a little tougher to say that after working for her, but I still believe it."

"People told me, 'You're crazy,' when I said I'd be in Bella's office," Tom, another intern, confides. "She's supposed to be so hard to work for."

"If you're really sensitive, it is," Jo Ellen says. "She does shout—"

The door opens, Bella leans out and shouts, "Ken, come in here!"

Jo Ellen and Tom look very busy while a tall young man on the full-time staff grabs up a sheaf of papers and lopes toward the private office. Although he closes the door after him, a rumble of unmistakable thunder comes through the wall.

"It's not calling you a name," Jo Ellen murmurs. "But she doesn't seem to care about your feelings. It's always, 'Why aren't you doing more, you dummy?' Nobody can ever do enough. I guess it's because she tries to do so much herself."

"She's great!" Tom insists. "This is the most exciting office on the Hill. In most other offices, interns spend eight hours every day opening envelopes. Here she really gives you something to do. We're all handling so much because she's involved in everything."

While he goes back to jotting notes summing up a Senate report about welfare reform, Christine at the reception desk is saying into her telephone, "No, this is one of her assistants, but may I take a message?" Rita, who works on scheduling, is telling another caller, "What she has indicated to me is that she is not accepting any more out-of-state speaking engagements until the end of the year, so I'd have to be pessimistic." A messenger from the majority leader's office is waiting to have some papers signed. The instant Ken emerges, looking harried but intent on getting back to his typewriter, the messenger is waved in. He comes out a minute later and so does Lee.

"Yes, this is a high intensity office," Lee agrees with the writer who has arranged to spend this day with the Congresswoman. "Bella's superproductive and superdynamic. Okay; if you want to go with her to her first committee, she's ready now."

And Bella herself, sighing mightily but also smiling at the same time, is suddenly standing there, too. "You want to know how many hats I have, I suppose," she says. "Come on, let's go."

The pace she sets striding toward the elevator forces anyone with her to participate in a walking race. She swings her shoulder forward as she takes each step, and every step covers a surprising distance. From the rear, for it is easy to fall behind, the effect undeniably is somewhat like an oversized duck waddling rapidly. More than a few photographers have been sufficiently struck by this view to take candid pictures of it, and these have infuriated Bella. "What are you doing?" she'll holler over her shoulder if she catches an individual with a camera following her. "Is my back interesting? Would you take somebody else's picture from behind?"

Such outbursts make her friends shake their heads. For news photographers are notoriously harsh with public figures, both male and female. Let a short man or a bald man run for office, and pictures are bound to turn up poking fun at their physical failing. Political cartoons are even more unkind, almost always seizing on some aspect of a person's appearance to mock. Yet Bella, who'd fiercely defend the feminist doctrine that looks aren't really important, just can't bear having her own appearance ridiculed.

"She feels it's some sort of plot," one of her oldest acquaintances surmises. "Like everybody, she has her own image of herself. She still thinks she looks like that gorgeous girl at Hunter."

Of course, she knows that she's gained some weight since then, but if anyone is brave enough to ask her about this, she gruffly blames it all on politics. "You can't eat right when you're going every minute," she says. "I put on forty pounds during my first campaign, and I haven't had the time to take it off." However, her family says that it happened more gradually, and that when she's in a turmoil she can't stick to a diet.

Still, her own opinion is bolstered repeatedly by people who've never seen her previously except on television. Now while she is striding to the elevator, she has an experience that occurs often, and she clearly enjoys it. Some visitors searching for the office of their own Representative change their course when they spot her, and surround her.

"I know you!" a woman exclaims. "I saw you on the Mike Douglas show, but your pictures don't do you justice—you're much better-looking in person."

Bella winks at the writer with her. "Who's your Congressman?" she asks expansively, as if she has nothing in the world she'd rather be doing than standing here chatting. "Oh, he's a pretty good guy; you're lucky to have him. My autograph? Why, sure." And she stands there signing her name till suddenly she claps a hand to her forehead. "I'll be late!" she says, swinging her shoulders as she resumes racing down the corridor.

By the time she reaches the hearing room a floor below her office, the session has indeed started. A witness from the Environmental Protection Agency is reading a statement supporting a proposed change in the procedure for issuing permits to companies that might pollute lakes or rivers. But she's actually timed her appearance as nearly as possible to coincide with the start of the questioning, for why should she listen to a statement one of her aides has already secured a copy of? If she didn't figure out short cuts like this, she'd never get through a day's work.

So instead of listening to something she's already read, she digs into her purse for some papers concerning the next hearing on her schedule. These she hasn't been able to go over yet. While the witness drones on, she swiftly turns page after page, slashing with a pencil to mark the important points. Her dark-rimmed eyeglasses—the small kind that are only for reading, and that let you look over them when you look straight ahead—her glasses slide lower and lower on her nose. Every minute or two she jams them up higher, or she glances around the room, or she shifts her position in her chair. No matter that she's obviously concentrating, she doesn't sit still as she studies.

But when she's finished this homework, she's even more fidgety. She rests her chin on a fist, she leans to whisper a comment to the man beside her, she rummages in her purse for a mirror and checks whether her hat needs adjusting. By now, the witness is answering questions from the chairman of this subcommittee. Nothing other than the dullest sort of detail interests these gentlemen, though, and nobody appears to be paying much attention to them. Many of the spectators seem nearly asleep.

"Does the gentlewoman from New York have any questions?"

This query from the chairman startles the audience because, according to the rules of seniority, several men should have their turns to examine the witness before Bella gets her chance. However, she's taken advantage of the conflict in her schedule to request and receive a special favor. There's a rustling as people come awake to watch Bella in action.

"I'd like to know," she starts calmly, "on what basis do you suggest that the granting of permits should be shifted from the federal to state level?"

"If you've read in our brief pamphlet—"

"I haven't read your brief pamphlet."

The witness looks a bit flustered but he goes on to say that various studies have indicated that state governments eventually will be able to take over the task under discussion.

"That's eventually," Bella says crisply. "But we have an act in effect now and why should we change it for something that may happen eventually?"

"We realize that there are some states that are not capable as of now. One would hope they would be able to step into the program as they develop."

"Have you checked that out with the states?" Bella asks, speaking more sharply now. "Do they like the idea?"

The witness sounds annoyed. "I haven't the foggiest notion," he says.

"Don't you think if you're proposing such a substantial change you ought to have the foggiest notion?" Bella demands.

"I'm not suggesting, *Ms.* Abzug," the man starts in a sarcastic tone, but whether he's angry because a woman is questioning him or just because he doesn't like this line of questioning, he forgets what he was going to say. "The certificate is the crux of the matter here," he starts again. "If the states give evidence of being able to take over, they ought to be allowed to do so."

Bella raises her eyebrows and sighs expressively. "I have no further questions at the moment," she murmurs, gathering up all of her papers and stuffing them back into her purse. An instant later, she's out in the hall where the lanky fellow from her office hands her a few new message slips.

"Ken," she says, after barely glancing at the messages, "I didn't have the proper questions for those water pollution experts. You're going to have to get me more material." Grabbing his arm, she drags him over to a bench, and they sit for a moment or two with their heads together. He takes rapid notes on a pad while she issues her instructions.

Then up on her feet again, she stomps off to the nearest elevator. "Damn thing isn't working," she mutters when the doors don't slide open the instant she pushes the button. "Can't be in three committees at once. Not even I can do that."

But she perks up immediately as a delegation of Asian women approach, shepherded by Jo Ellen from her office.

"This is Mrs. Kanita from Thailand," Jo Ellen says somewhat apprehensively.

"Hi! How are you?" Bella beams upon the foreign guests, and Jo Ellen, looking relieved, explains that Mrs. Kanita is chairperson of the status of women's groups writing a women's rights clause they hope will be included in their country's new constitution.

"How's it coming?" Bella asks. "Are you getting much support?" And she listens intently for several minutes while she receives a summary of the legal position of women in Thailand. "Oh, that's interesting," she says. "I'm really glad to know you have some women lawyers over there. I practiced law about twenty-five years before I came to Congress, but I don't practice now even though plenty of men here do because I regard that as a conflict of interest. Which reminds me, I do have a hearing going on right this minute. No, it's my pleasure, and if there's anything I can do to help, any data you'd like, don't hesitate to ask my office. Now I'm sorry I'm in such a rush . . . " And waving cheerfully, she darts onto an elevator just as the doors open. "Whew!" she says, glancing at her watch.

In the room where the mass transit subcommittee is meeting, Bella's mere appearance creates an audible stir. Like most similar sessions conducting the routine business of the government, this one has not the slightest aura of history about it. Seven or eight nondescript men sit at intervals along a polished table facing smaller tables for witnesses and the press, and about twenty rows of seats for spectators. While important changes in policy regarding the spending of federal money are often debated during such hearings, the tone is usually so muted that most people who aren't experts on the subject being discussed find themselves bored. It takes a Bella to infuse a little excitement, as she proceeds to do when she questions the head of New York City's public transportation system.

First she leads him on to list the many problems the city has in trying to finance transit improvements. Then he begins to look uncomfortable while

Congresswoman Abzug has to hold onto her hat as she debarks from a helicopter on her way to attend a hearing on New York City transit problems. *Courtesy New York City Transportation Administration*

she asks him about point after point in the proposed bill the subcommittee is considering. How would this clause help? Or this one? Or even this one? He has come here to defend the bill, but under Bella's prodding he's proving instead that such a bill really wouldn't do much good.

"So it's not enough, is it?" Bella says. "We're still continuing a process that's the wrong process. Why shouldn't we have the security in mass transit of a trust fund?" Now she's hammering on the table with a fist, and her voice has grown much louder. "Why should only the interstate highways be funded with a trust fund? This is what I find is the basic difficulty in the bill before this committee. Nobody wants to bite the bullet!"

Smiling faintly as if he's surprised himself, the witness says, "I'm willing to bite the bullet."

Bella smiles back at him triumphantly. Though the uninformed may not realize it, she's just scored an important point, and she still looks happy as she gathers up her papers again to go on to her next committee meeting. There she'll read her statement that she worked on with Lee last night; then if her luck holds, she can join Ron Dellums and some of the other black activists for a quick lunch in the House Dining Room—assuming she'll even make it to their table, for whenever she walks through that doorway, the rankest reactionaries come running to ask her to shake the hand of their niece or daughter. Funny how these guys keep sneering at her, she says, but they still turn somersaults to get her to say hello to their own kids. You'd think it might occur to them that young people had some reason for admiring Bella Abzug.

After lunch, she'll have to check her office again, maybe sneaking in a few phone calls before racing for the House itself. A couple of tricky amendments are coming up this afternoon, so she'll probably have to stay on the floor till around five thirty. She has a nearly perfect record as far as being counted on every roll call is concerned, and she wants to keep it that way. How those goof-offs who miss about fifty per cent of the votes can face the people who've elected them is something she'll never understand. Sure, she'd like to disappear for a swim in the House gym's pool, now that she's got them to set aside time for women. She desperately needs to have her hair done, too, but is this why she's been sent to Washington?

Then by six o'clock, she'll definitely have to sit down with that writer and act as if nobody's ever asked her before why she's in politics. Good lord! Make her be patient, until she can start tackling the really hard part of the day. What with the length of Lee's list already, they'll be at it beyond midnight.

At some point they'll phone out for a steak and a salad, and she'll also steal ten minutes to talk to Martin. But otherwise it'll be pure drudgery, wading through a sea of documents, planning strategy, and trying to reach all sorts of people who could make a difference if they'd only listen to her.

For Bella in her second term is no less intent on shaking up the system than she was when she first entered Congress, but now it's not as easy to keep track of her activities. Like the government itself, she's still very visible—wherever you look on Capitol Hill, you stand a good chance of seeing her. And yet,

Back on the Hill 145

she's operating much more effectively behind the scenes.

The basic reason is certainly not a mystery. From the instant this new Congress convened, something amazing has been happening in Washington. Overshadowing all else during Bella's second term, a more fantastic drama than anybody could have imagined has been unfolding week by week before the astounded eyes of the whole world. The downfall of Richard Nixon! Nothing like it has ever occurred in nearly two centuries of American history.

Throughout the spring of 1973, hints of what was to come have thrilled Bella. No, she's not surprised by the Watergate revelations, for she's suspected Nixon and his cronies all along. Should she jump in immediately and file a new impeachment resolution based on what John Dean has been telling the newspapers? She wants to—but she listens when people like "Tip" O'Neill, the House majority leader, urge her to hold back.

Wait, they say, wait till we see what comes out at the Senate hearing this summer. Then, in an ordinary hearing room on the other side of the Capitol, the most outrageous facts ever to be divulged about a President of the United States spellbind millions of people watching television, and Bella can hardly stand not doing something.

But wait, they tell her again; wait till the country is prepared for such a drastic step as impeachment. And Bella waits during a winter while that man in the White House seems to seal his own doom by firing the special prosecutor he has promised to cooperate with and by withholding evidence from the House committee that is finally considering whether or not there are grounds for impeaching this President.

Month after month Bella rages with impatience, but she waits—because she knows that Bella Abzug can do more for her country by keeping silent now than by raising her voice. Near the end of her first term, she'd been severely hurt when a group of researchers working for Ralph Nader had issued a report giving her an awful slap in the face. Those Nader kids were her kind of people, strong supporters of the same reforms she believed in, and they'd softened the blow by applauding her program. But they'd really wounded her with the remark that her way of speaking up was so abrasive that any measure having her name attached to it automatically lost thirty to forty votes on the floor of the House.

Furthermore, that campaign against Ryan had dealt a worse blow. The votes the Nader group was talking about were mainly right-wing reactionaries who'd oppose a liberal bill most of the time, no matter what name was on it. But in the Ryan primary, a couple of dozen Democrats, including more than a few liberals, had contributed money from their own pockets toward defeating her. That wasn't how the game was usually played. Congressmen very rarely took sides openly in a contest between two incumbents.

So they thought she was a headline-grabber, or maybe they just hated strong-minded women. Too bad!

And yet in her second term, Bella gets somebody else to sponsor a mass transit amendment that's bound to irritate the highway people. Of course, she's not about to soft-pedal any of her real aims. But during all of those tense months while the Nixon White House is under siege, while this man she hates is finally forced to resign, Congresswoman Abzug pours her energy into a lot of much less exciting activity on Capitol Hill. If a reporter asks her to comment about some new development in the great drama absorbing the public, she does so rather quietly.

Quietly for Bella, that is. Then, in the autumn of 1974, she has an easy time winning a third term.

12

And What Next?

It is 1976 and President Ford is in the White House, and a funny thing has happened to Bella Abzug.

She's been right about Vietnam, which is finally just a bad memory. She's been right about Nixon, who's exiled behind the fence of his California estate. But on Capitol Hill, when the House majority leader gets asked what he thinks of Bella these days, "Tip" O'Neill says:

"She's changed, no question about it. When she first came here, she had a chip on her shoulder. Now she's one of the most popular members of the House. She's a factor."

That tickles Bella, and yet she feels obliged to set the record straight. "You have to understand what's gone on since I've been here," she says. "I came out

Congresswoman Abzug at one of the many committee meetings she must attend. *Dev O'Neill photo*

of the peace movement and women's rights. They thought I was a lunatic. Now these causes are being supported by a majority of the people. I've been out in front. Everybody's caught up."

However, there's no disputing one fact. In the *Chicago Tribune,* where political figures from New York are not generally admired, a long magazine article near the end of 1975 is devoted to examining Bella's career, and it reports:

> After five years in national politics and despite a certain softening that has gone virtually unperceived by her national following, Bella Abzug has become more than a politician the way John Wayne is more than an actor and Joe Namath is more than a jock. She has emerged from the ranks of the semi-famous to become an All-American superstar.

Even her political enemies, and she still has plenty of those, admit her superstardom. Practically anywhere in the country, practically everyone immediately recognizes a picture of her. When she shakes her finger at the head of the CIA as he admits that his agency has broken the law by spying on her and other Americans, even some conservatives urge, "Give 'em hell, Bella." Although many people can neither spell nor pronounce her last name, that doesn't matter. Like "Jackie," or "Cher," or just a

And What Next?

handful of other celebrities, her first name is enough to identify her.

Such unquestioned fame gives some of Bella's warmest supporters a great idea. "Why don't you run for President?" they ask her. When she winds up one of her rousing speeches, somebody in the audience will probably pump her hand enthusiastically and come out with the same question. If she's talking to a stranger, Bella will grin and say, "I'm glad you agree with my mother." For she still finds this is the easiest way to dispose of the query, even after her mother's death late in 1975 at the ripe age of eighty-eight.

At least a few devoted fans seriously think she ought to try for the White House. Her own husband, though, despite his jokes about becoming First Man, doesn't expect this honor, not merely because politics don't particularly interest him. "That's not my bag," he says. Nevertheless, he has his opinions, among them the positive conviction that his wife won't seek the presidency. Why not?

"Very simple," he says. "She's Jewish. I personally believe that maybe in ten years we might have a woman president, but I think anti-Semitism is so deeply ingrained in this country that we won't have a Jewish President for a lot longer than that." Still, he shrugs and admits he's often been wrong about political issues, and he might be wrong about this too.

Most experts don't think so, however. They note that when Bella first went to the House of Represen-

Bella Abzug with President Jacqueline Wexler of Hunter College, receiving an honorary doctorate of laws in June 1975. *Hunter College photo*

tatives, quite a point was made of her religion. People who were proud of her as well as people who hated her thought it was important to mention that she was the first Jewish woman ever to serve in Congress. After a while somebody remembered, though, that this distinction really belonged to Florence P. Kahn, a California Republican who'd entered the House via the traditional widow's route in 1925 and then had been re-elected to several terms in her own right.

In any case, Bella's religious background has gradually ceased to seem worthy of comment as long as she's in a Congress where twenty-one of the members, including three of the eighteen women, are of the same faith. She's also become less lonely politically, with a new crop of younger and more liberal Representatives giving her some staunch new allies. Even among the old-timers, she's finally earned a good measure of respect and affection. "She does her homework," the serious lawmakers say approvingly. "When you tell her a joke, she doesn't give you a blank stare like some of those sourpuss reformers," according to easygoing conservatives. "She laughs!"

In the press gallery, where boredom is an occupational disease, Bella has few rivals. "You can't believe how deadly dull most of the guys here are," a veteran writer sighs. "But you can always count on her to liven things up." Not that a colorful personality guarantees uncritical approval from the media, for Capitol Hill correspondents take a special pride in their ability to deflate political egos, and they also like to prove how sharp they are. So their verdict on Bella tends to be mixed, for instance:

"She's one of the driving forces here, but she goes overboard all the time." Or:

"She's a monumental pain, but she's been right!"

With nobody neutral about her, it's easy to start a

debate on the topic: What has Bella really accomplished?

"She's sponsored more creative legislation than anyone else," an experienced woman journalist says crisply. "On child care, women's rights, welfare reform."

"Sponsored," a pipe-smoking columnist says in a sarcastic tone. "Anybody can introduce any sort of bill, but it's another matter to get it passed. Except for a couple of amendments here and there, she's been a flop as a legislator."

"How can you say that?" a New York writer demands. "Abzug-sponsored legislation has brought over four billion dollars to New York State in federal grants for badly needed public works programs and cleaning up water pollution—and she's kept plenty of bad bills from sneaking through. The *Times* and the *Daily News* don't agree on much politically, but they've both run editorials complimenting Bella on watching out so carefully for the city's interests."

"And she's got equal pay for women into several important spending bills," the woman writer adds. "Besides, she's the most effective spokesperson the feminist cause has ever had here."

"Nonsense!" says the pipe-smoker. "She's the symbol of the far left, and a great many women don't identify with her at all."

"She's a symbol, all right," a young man from one of the TV networks says. "You might call her the unofficial leader for everybody in the country who hasn't been getting a fair shake up until now. Thank God for Bella!" Then he grins. "But thank God there's only one of her, or we'd all go deaf."

"You just can't stand a woman who speaks up," one of this man's feminine colleagues says. It's an open secret that these two are constantly fighting each other for air time. "You know perfectly well anyway," the woman correspondent adds, "everything that's really important around here gets decided behind the scenes, and Bella may be the only woman who's ever figured out how to get listened to there. In three terms, she's got more influence than a lot of men who've been around thirty years."

On that point, many observers seem to agree. It also appears fairly clear that if Bella wants to stay in Congress, it will be hard to defeat her.

What would she say her main accomplishments have been so far?

"My leadership in the anti-war movement, in and out of Congress," she starts. "My leadership in forming the women's political movement." She pauses, looking dismayed. "I don't want to sound conceited," she says, "but I seem to have had the vision to see what was evil earlier than most and to speak out against it earlier than most. Well, maybe I didn't see it so much sooner. But I spoke out sooner. I mean, I was fighting for civil liberties in the 1950s and I'll bet there were no more than a hundred lawyers in the entire country who would take those cases then. My whole thing about becoming a lawyer was to fight against injustice, to fight for the ordinary man and woman."

She stops a minute, then goes on with a slight smile.

"I'm considered one of the most radical people in the Congress," she says. "But actually I'm an idealist. I really believe in the Constitution. I've fought for it ever since I can remember."

And Bella Abzug obviously intends to keep right on fighting the same battle, no matter where the next stage of her career may take her. For even if her future can't be predicted, the record of her past proves this point.

After just her first year in politics, she was once asked if there was anything she wished she'd done differently.

"No," Bella said. "But I should have done more of it."

Suggested for Further Reading

Abzug, Bella, *Bella! Ms. Abzug Goes to Washington*, edited by Mel Ziegler. New York: Saturday Review Press, 1972.

Chamberlin, Hope, *Minority of Members: Women in the U.S. Congress 1917–72*. New York: Praeger, 1973; paperback, New American Library, 1974.

Faber, Doris, *Petticoat Politics: How American Women Won the Right to Vote*. New York: Lothrop, Lee & Shepard, 1967.

Fleming, Alice, *The Senator from Maine: Margaret Chase Smith*. New York: Thomas Y. Crowell, 1969.

Haskins, James, *Fighting Shirley Chisholm*. New York: Dial Press, 1975.

Johnson, Gerald W., *The Congress.* New York: William Morrow, 1963.
Liston, Robert A., *Politics from Precinct to Presidency.* New York: Delacorte Press, 1968.
Warren, Ruth, *A Pictorial History of Women in America.* New York: Crown, 1975.

NOTE: It should be added that newspapers and magazines offer the best source of current information about Bella Abzug, and that this book has been based on personal interviews supplemented by material in the files of such periodicals.

D. F.

Index

Abzug, Eve Gail (Egee), 6, 49, 57, 59–60, 66–67, 75, 94, 116–117
Abzug, Isobel Jo (Liz), 56–57, 59–60, 66–67, 75–76, 80–81, 116–117
Abzug, Martin, 31–33, 39–43, 45–49, 53–54, 56–57, 59–60, 66–67, 69, 74–75, 92, 94, 101–103, 117–120, 126, 144
accomplishments, Bella's, 153–156
anti-Semitism, 12–13, 151
Armed Services Committee, 98–99, 103, 107
arms race, 62, 64, 69–70
Aunt Janet, 30, 32–33, 41

black activists, 71–72, 77, 143
block-busting, 57–59, 67
Boston University, 116
Bronx, the, 10, 12, 18, 22, 25, 56

Capitol Hill, 3, 96, 107, 130, 133, 148, 152–153
Caruso, Enrico, 14
Catskills, the, 36
Chicago Tribune, 150
Chisholm, Shirley, 97, 110
CIA, 150
civil-rights cases, 47, 50–55, 155
Clinton, De Witt (high school), 21
Coe, John, 55

Columbia, 30, 34–36, 42–43
Communism, 48–50, 53, 70, 72, 79, 89
Congress, Ninety-second, 95–99, 103–111
Conservative party, 128
Czechoslovakia, 48

Daily News, 118, 153
day-care centers, 92, 110
Dean, John, 145
Dellums, Ron, 143
Democratic caucus, 104
Democratic convention (1968), 77–78
Democratic party, 76–79, 82–84, 86, 97, 104, 111, 113, 120, 125–127
Depression, the, 25
Douglas, Helen Gahagan, 79
Douglas, Mike, 137

Eisenhower, President Dwight, 62
England (Great Britain), 48, 62–63, 69
Environmental Protection Agency, 137
Equal Rights Amendment, 110

Farber, Barry, 86
Farbstein, Congressman Leonard, 82–84
Ford, President Gerald, 148
Friedman, Dora, 133

Germany, Nazi, 27, 108
Government Operations Committee, 103–104
Greenwich Village, 67–69, 92

Harlem, 36, 97
Harvard, 29–30
hats, Bella's, 4, 6–7, 95–96, 102–103, 135
Hebrew school, 16
Hicks, Louise Day, 101–102
High School of Music and Art, 67, 75–76
Hofstra, 75, 116
Humphrey, Vice-President Hubert, 78
Hunter, 24–25, 27, 30, 34, 36, 45, 81, 89, 96, 136

Inner Circle, 118–120

Japan, 12, 26, 62
Johnson, President Lyndon, 72, 76–77

Kaddish, 19
Kahn, Florence P., 152
Kelber, Mim, 81, 133
Kennedy, Mrs. John F., 65–66
Kennedy, President John F., 64, 78, 88
Khruschev, Mrs. Nikita, 65–66
Kingsbridge Jewish Center, 16, 20

Index

Liberal party, 127
Life magazine, 114
Lindsay, Mayor John, 118
Little Italy, 36
Live and Let Live Meat Market, The, 13–14
Lower East Side, the, 12

MacLaine, Shirley, 127
Malcolm X, 67
McCarthy, Senator Joseph, 49
McCarthyism, 49–50
McGee, Willie, 50–55
McGovern, Senator George, 126–127
McGrory, Mary, 99–101
Menuhin, Yehudi, 31
Miller, "Fishbait," 95–96
Mount Vernon, N.Y., 57–59, 66–67

Nader, Ralph, 146
New Deal, 22–23, 44, 79
New York City, 8–10, 12, 18, 22, 24–26, 30, 32, 34–37, 41–42, 49, 56, 64–70, 76–77, 82–88, 92, 112–113, 121, 123, 125, 127, 141
New York Post, 84
New York Times, The, 54–55, 110–111, 153
Newsweek magazine, 126
Nixon, Pat, 102–103

Nixon, President Richard, 78–79, 96–97, 102–103, 105, 107–109, 116, 122–124, 126–127, 145–147, 148
Novick, Lee, 131, 133, 135 143–144

O'Neill, "Tip," 145, 148

peace movement, the, 63, 69–74, 76–78, 105, 149–150, 154
peace oath, 97
peace resolution, 97, 103–104
Pearl Harbor, 29
Pentagon, 70, 72, 90
poker, 37–38
Poland, 49
Public Works Committee, 103–104

Republican party, 78, 85–86, 92, 111, 123, 128, 152
"resolution of inquiry," 105–106
Robert's Rules of Order, 29
Rockefeller, Nelson, 113, 125
Roosevelt, President Franklin D., 22, 44, 83
Russell, Bertrand, 63
Russia, 12–13
Ryan, Priscilla, 127–128
Ryan, William Fitts (Bill), 121–128, 146

Sabbath, 14
Savitzky, Emanuel (Manny), 12–14, 19–20, 22–23
Savitzky, Esther Tanklefsky, 12–14, 16, 20, 22–24, 29–30, 34–35, 40, 87, 94, 116, 151
Savitzky, Helene, 13–14, 18, 20, 24, 116
Scott, Senator Hugh, 109
Seventh Avenue Story, 46
Simpson, Carole, 7–8
Socialist Workers party, 128
Soviet Union, 53, 61–62, 69
Steinem, Gloria, 125, 129
stock market crash (1929), 22
stockings, silk, 26
Streisand, Barbra, 87
strontium 90, 61
synagogue, 15–16, 19

Tanklefsky, Esther, *See* Savitzky, Esther Tanklefsky
Tanklefsky, Grandma, 13–14
Tanklefsky, Grandpa, 13–16, 18–19
test ban treaty, nuclear, 69
tests, nuclear bomb, 61–62, 65

Uncle Hymie, 41
Uncle Julius, 30, 32–33, 41–42
union movement, 44–45, 71–72

United Nations, 64–65

Vietnam, 70, 72–73, 77, 83–84, 97, 102, 105, 115, 148
Village Voice, 122
Von Hoffman, Nicholas, 112–113

Wall Street Journal, 122
Walton (high school), 21, 23–25, 81
Washington Post, 84, 112–113
Watergate, 145–147
wedding, Bella and Martin's, 40–42
Willett, Roslyn, 125
Williams, Alice, 49, 59–60
Wilson, Dagmar, 63, 66
Wilson, President Woodrow, 13
Women for McGovern, 127
Women Strike for Peace, the (WSP), 63–64, 71, 73, 81, 97
women's liberation movement, 77, 88, 110, 115, 119, 123, 149–150, 153–154
Women's Political Caucus, 110, 125, 129–130
World War I, 13
World War II, 25–26, 29–30, 37–38, 44–45, 72–73

Zionism, 17

About the Author

Doris Faber, who has written many books for young readers, is the author of *Petticoat Politics: How American Women Won the Right to Vote* and *Oh, Lizzie! The Life of Elizabeth Cady Stanton* as well as several biographies of Presidents. A former reporter for *The New York Times* who covered many political stories, she now lives on a farm in upstate New York, writing books and articles and devoting much of her time to growing vegetables. She is married to Harold Faber, an editor and author, and is the mother of two college-age daughters.

IMC
921
Ab998f
c.1

396048

INSTRUCTIONAL MEDIA CENTER
William D. McIntyre Library
University of Wisconsin
Eau Claire, Wisconsin